BUILDING A FIBERGLASS BOAT

ARTHUR EDMUNDS

Editor: John P. O'Connor, Jr.

BRISTOL FASHION PUBLICATIONS, INC
Harrisburg, Pennsylvania

Building A Fiberglass Boat by Arthur Edmunds

Published by Bristol Fashion Publications, Inc.

ISBN: 1-892216-16-7
LCCN: 99-072380

Contribution acknowledgments

Cover Photo: 47 foot, 42 knot sportfisherman designed and photographed by Arthur Edmunds.
Inside Graphics/Photos: by Arthur Edmunds, unless otherwise indicated.
Cover Design: John P. Kaufman.

INTRODUCTION

There are many people who read boating magazines, or crew with boat owners for fishing, or enjoy a relaxing afternoon cruise. These people are well informed about boats for sale and they go to boat shows to inquire about what is new on the market. Often these experienced people become boat owners by building their boat exactly as they want it. Many times they cannot find what they want from the many manufacturers. All it takes is time and energy and less of an investment when compared with boats from the dealers.

This book is written for those people who know what they want in a boat and have a great amount of satisfaction in their workmanship. Glass fiber hulls have become dominant in the boating world as the most desirable material. By far, longevity is the most important quality of glass fiber laminates. Boats built in 1950 are still being used with great success. That is why this book concentrates solely on this durable and popular material. Any conceivable shape can be made from glass fiber when laminating a custom hull. The building techniques are explained in these pages.

Glass fiber laminates are man-made products that are a combination of the glass fiber filaments and a binder of resin. As such, the quality of the finished hull depends solely on the patience and skill of the person who builds it. The skill of laminating is very easily acquired with a little practice on some sample laminates. Like any other piece of workmanship, it is the careful attention to detail that results in a fine looking and long lasting boat. Boat building cannot be done in a quick and haphazard manner. Concentration and perseverance must be judiciously applied to obtain the boat of your lifetime.

As you read these pages, you will soon understand the many tasks and time involved in a boat building project. You may decide building your own boat is not a project you have the time to complete yourself, even if this is your decision, you will have the knowledge to contract the project to a competent builder, confident you will have the boat of your dreams when the project is complete.

Arthur Edmunds

TABLE OF CONTENTS

CHAPTER ONE
WHY BUILD YOUR OWN BOAT?

Many people who go out on boats want to own their own boat but can't justify the expense in this era of inflated prices. This book will discuss the alternative solution of building your own glass fiber boat, either when buying a bare hull or when building a custom hull. The book will illustrate a boat about 25 to 33 feet in length. But the construction procedures apply to hulls of any length.

One exception is when a boat smaller than twenty feet is considered. The stock boat market is literally flooded with small boats and because of the large numbers, the prices are very competitive and it often is practical to purchase rather than build. If you think building a small hull is absolutely necessary, it is easier to work quarter-inch plywood into the desired shape and use it as a core material. Glass is then laminated both inside and outside to the desired thickness, neglecting the plywood thickness. There are many inexpensive plans and frame kits for small boats and this is probably the least expensive path to follow. Another option is rebuilding a good used hull.

When you look at what is available in manufactured boats, you see open boats for fishing, water skiing or family outings, plus semi-enclosed boats, sport fishing boats or cruising hulls. Many times an owner will want something different, such as a wide open deck for SCUBA diving groups or for fish traps, a deck crane for salvage operations or a tall mast for communications antennae. If you want one of these arrangements or a boat with different berthing facilities or equipment, it may be wise to build it yourself.

Pride of ownership and knowing that you built it yourself; these are great stimuli for building your boat. If you want it done right, build it yourself. When you do your own construction you can control the costs, quality and amount of equipment.

A custom boat always commands a higher price on the resale market, rightly assuming that the hull is of top quality and that careful attention to detail has been paid in all phases of the design and construction. In any port, the custom hull gets the most attention and inquiries.

WHERE TO BUILD

Often an owner will select a boat less than 25 feet, as that is the space available in the average garage. This selection of a building site is very important as the rental of a warehouse can run into many thousands over the time necessary for construction. Also, one of the first considerations must be the last step of getting the boat to a launching site. Smaller boats can be put directly on a trailer, but larger hulls must be set in a cradle (described later) and lifted onto a flatbed transport. Wires above roads must not be between the building site and the water, as this will create an overhead clearance problem.

Wherever you select, make sure the neighbors will not mind the noise of construction and the occasional smell of styrene from the resin used in laminations. There will be many hours devoted to sanding and the dust should be contained so the neighbor's roses will not be contaminated. Security must be considered at any building site as the theft of tools or engines can occur anywhere. Padlocks on the doors are not adequate, but dead bolts are more secure. Windows should be barred or pinned, as the glass is easily broken. Of course, the door opening should be wider and higher than the boat.

If you cannot borrow or rent a suitable building site,

some people consider a temporary building shelter made of pipe frames plus wire supports held by ground anchors. The pipe may be galvanized steel or PVC, which is usually covered with a sheet of plastic both inside and outside the pipe. These shelters are advertised in the magazines devoted to boat building, or they may be built by a clever mechanic.

Sometimes, with friendly cooperation, a lean-to type of shelter may be built outside an existing building so one wall is common to both. The obvious disadvantage to a temporary shelter is it cannot be locked and there is absolutely no security. High winds may destroy the plastic covering and heavy rains may flood the building site. The temperature for laminating successfully must be between 65 degrees and 85 degrees, which may be difficult to attain in a temporary shelter.

You now see the requirements for a building site. It must be large enough to house the boat in all three dimensions, plus room for a workbench, table saw, dry glass material storage and safe resin storage.

THE COST OF DOING BUSINESS

Building your boat is a very pleasurable occupation as we all get a great satisfaction from a job well done. But lurking in the shadows is the consideration of money. Costs have to be considered in whatever we do. I have compiled a list of approximate costs of a manufactured boat and a boat built by an owner. These are estimates as there is a wide variation from builder to builder. The greatest difference is in the type and horsepower of engines that are installed. Obviously there is a great difference from a small outboard motor, to inboard gas engines, to large diesel engines. A varnished, rare wood interior may be three times the cost of painted plywood. A 25-foot stock boat may be $30,000 or $60,000 and a 33-foot manufactured boat may be $110,000 or $160,000. When comparing boat prices, pay careful attention to the engines and the extent and quality of the interior.

COST ESTIMATE FOR A 33-FOOT GLASS MANUFACTURED BOAT

	POWERBOAT		SAILBOAT	
Items	Hours	Materials	Hours	Materials
Hull	120	5,250	120	5,250
Deck	120	3,750	120	3,750
Mold Costs (2)		2,150		2,150
Bulkheads	80	420	80	420
Framing	80	650	80	650
Diesels (2)	4	28,110	4	8,110
Mounts & Batt.	16	198	8	217
Control & Steer	8	410	4	182
Stuffing Box	8	485	8	185
Shaft & Strut	16	620	8	290
Props & Rudder	78	590	14	445
Exhaust	32	420	16	230
Alignment	26	120	18	60
Tanks	32	1,950	32	900
Electrical	80	1,650	80	1,650
Plumbing	88	1,070	88	1,070
Install Deck	32	180	32	180
Lifelines	64	2,600	96	5,600
Hatch & Cleats	48	1,330	64	2,500
Windows	32	1,950	32	950
Instruments	32	850	32	700
Deck Seats	32	950	32	820
Berths	80	350	80	350
Head	80	950	80	950
Lockers	32	280	32	280
Galley	80	1,820	80	1,820
Dining Table	32	700	32	700
Hull Covering	80	620	80	620
Headliner	80	850	80	850
Ballast			80	5,000
Mast & Rigging			32	9,500
Labor Total	1,492		1,544	
Material Total		61,313		56,879
Labor Cost @ $12.00/hr	17,904		18,528	
Total Cost		79,177		74,907

TOTAL COSTS ESTIMATE FOR A MANUFACTURED POWERBOAT

Labor and Materials (33-foot)	$79,177
Employee Benefits	13,000
Plant Overhead Expenses	12,000
Insurance	1,633
Advertising & Dealer Programs	950
Transport	<u>1,840</u>
Manufacturing Cost	$108,600
Manufacturing Profit	9,200
Dealer Discount, before expenses	<u>25,000</u>
Advertised Retail Price	$142,800

The primary purpose of listing these costs is only for comparison with costs of building your boat and to see exactly where your money will be spent. These costs must be determined before the project is started.

COST ESTIMATE OF OWNER BUILT 25 & 33-FOOT POWERBOAT

Procedure	25-FOOT Hours	25-FOOT Materials	33-FOOT Hours	33-FOOT Materials
Build Hull Plug	100	500	120	500
Laminate hull	240	2,800	240	5,500
Sand & Paint	200	500	240	1 500
Turn Over & Cradle	70	1,500	80	1,500
Deck Framing	40	500	40	500
Laminate Deck	100	1,000	120	2,500
Sand & Paint	130	200	142	1,500
Tanks & Piping	40	2,000	40	2,000
Electrical	80	800	80	1,800
Plumbing	80	500	80	1 000
Place Two Diesels	4	28,000	4	28,000
Mounts/Batteries	40	530	48	530
Steer & controls	12	900	12	1,400
Exhaust & Stuffing Box	40	1,000	40	1,000
Shafts & Struts	16	620	16	620
Props & Rudders	60	500	76	600
Bulkheads & Framing	150	800	180	1,000
Engine Alignment	30	120	30	120
Windows & Ports.	40	500	80	2,000
Deck/Hull Joint & Rails	80	500	80	1,000
Instruments	40	500	40	1,000
Lifelines & Rails	40	500	80	1,500
Hatches & Doors	40	600	40	600
Berths	80	350	80	350
Head & Shower	40	400	80	600
Lockers & Drawers	32	300	32	300
Galley	40	500	80	900
Dining Area	40	200	40	700
Interior Covering	100	500	160	1,000
Total Labor	1,956		2,380	
Material Cost w/2 Diesel Engines		47,620		61,520
Cost w/o Engines		19,620		33,520
Cost with two outboards		30,000		44,000
Plus overhead			Variable	

Depending on whether you rent, borrow or build an area for the boat construction, you will have overhead costs in addition to the above listed estimated costs. These may be small if you are in your own garage completing all the work yourself; or as much as $15,000 if you rent a building, have some paid labor and pay for the moving of the completed boat to the launching site. Don't forget additional insurance -- especially fire -- and theft and the utility bills.

In looking at the construction costs for an owner built boat, you must realize that the man-hours required vary widely. Some people work very quickly and are well organized, while others like to work slowly and with precision. The hours and costs for engine and mechanical installations are quite close on all boats of the same size as you must install the engine, exhaust, shafts, propeller struts and rudders in a correct manner in all types of hulls. There are no cost-cutting areas when discussing mechanical systems. You can reduce costs by having only one engine, no AC generator and a minimum of equipment. The primary area where costs can be reduced is in the interior, which will be discussed in a later chapter.

The total number of hours required for building your boat is much higher than for a manufacturer because the workers on a production line can perform their repetitive work in a shorter time once they have become familiar with that specific task. A manufacturing plant has the tools and material ready at the work station, where the custom builder must spend time locating and buying the material. Since the manufacturer buys material in large quantities, they can buy at a reduced price, called OEM (Original Equipment Manufacturer). The individual must buy at a retailer if buying only one or two items and cannot obtain the thirty to fifty percent discounts available only to the manufacturers.

As seen on the cost charts, the manufacturing cost of a 33-foot sailboat and powerboat are very close. The additional cost of the ballast, mast, boom and rigging is offset by the reduced cost of one, small diesel engine. The sailboat's sails and deck winches are not included in these costs, which by themselves may add up to $25,000. Electronics on either power or sailboats may add another $25,000. AC generators and galley appliances greatly increase the costs of all types of boats.

ENGINE SELECTION

The chart of building costs shows a great variance depending on the engine cost and hard thought should be given to your exact requirements and what is the minimum expenditure. If you are going to use your boat for recreational purposes, usually less than 500 hours each year, gasoline inboard or outboard engines may be the best option. If you will be operating a commercial boat, probably more than one thousand hours per year, a diesel engine is warranted.

Whether you install one or two engines, is a matter of personal preference and the desired operating speed. Two diesel engines are shown in the above cost estimates just for the purposes of equal comparison. From the viewpoint of both economy and safety, a single inboard or outboard engine, with a small outboard engine alongside, might prove to be a viable option. The small outboard would be used only in an emergency or for very slow trolling if you are fishing.

Boat speed is usually the one number that an owner has in mind for his boat. Water skiing may require a maximum speed of 30 knots but family cruising may need only 15 knots. Speed is dependent on the total engine advertised horsepower and the total weight of the boat as it will be operated. Boat weight must include people on board, fuel, water and all the gear and food that the crew brings. The higher the speed, the more expensive the boat.

The above cost estimates use a *25* and 33-foot boat as examples and I will continue with the same lengths. The 25-foot boat will have a total weight of about 6000 pounds and the 33-foot boat will weigh about 15,000 pounds. The following chart shows which total horsepower engines will be required for a specific speed.

Total Horsepower	Knots @ 6000 Pounds	Knots @ 15000 Pounds
50	15	10
75	18	12
100	22	15
125	24	16
150	27	17
200	31	20
400	44	28

BUYING A BARE HULL

Sometimes you can find a glass hull that fits the requirements for your boat. If the quality is acceptable, it may be a good investment, as it will save many hours of building a plug and hull sanding or building a mold, as described later. You should ask the following about a bare hull:

a. Is the hull designed for the speed I require?

b. Is the hull designed for the engines amidships or aft?

c. Is a deck molding available that will fit or could be modified for my requirements? Is there a set of drawings available?

d. Is the style of hull and deck to my liking?

e. Can the builder show me the thickness and content of the laminate?

f. Can I contact other owners who have bought and built from this hull?

g. How can I transport this hull to my building site? At what cost?

Some boat repair yards and some smaller manufacturers will sell a bare hull and sometimes a glass deck molding that has been designed for the hull. If you talk with owners that have purchased this hull, you will find the good points and problems they have experienced. Generally, you should be able to buy a bare hull for about the same cost as your labor and materials, plus a reasonable profit. It may be difficult to locate a suitable bare hull in some sections of the country. They are usually advertised in the classified ad section of the boating magazines for people building their own boats. Boat yards, small boat builders, brokers, surveyors and designers may know of sources for the builders of bare hulls.

If you want a boat that will have a speed over 12 knots, you will want a V-bottom hull rather than round bottom. The aft portion of the chine (intersection of hull bottom and hull sides), as seen in profile, should be horizontal or slope down slightly from the horizontal as it runs from amidships to the stem. Boats that will operate at less than 12 knots will have less resistance with a round bottom shape.

There is always the question of hull materials and thickness when buying a bare hull. The answers should be provided by the builder. If the thickness of a hull is minimum, laminate can always be added on the inside, but the cost of this strengthening must be added to the hull cost.

The laminator of the hull should show a laminate sample from a hole that was cut for a through hull fitting. This will verify the thickness and show alternating layers of glass mat and woven roving were used throughout. Adequate hull thickness depends on the boat weight and the speed at which it will operate. This factor is calculated by the designer for each hull. This thickness should be shown on your drawings for the hull sides, hull bottom and keel areas. The thickness of the keel should be carried the full length of the boat for twelve inches each side of centerline and up the stem and transom to the deck level.

If the boat will be used for commercial fishing or hauling cargo, the hull should be twenty-five percent thicker than a recreational craft. Generally, the thickness at the sheer should not be less than one-quarter of an inch and the bottom thickness should be twice the hull side thickness. The keel is a minimum of four times the hull side thickness.

Considering the 25-foot and 33-foot boats, the 25-foot hull should have a hull side thickness of at least 0.25 inches, a bottom thickness of 0.50 inches and a keel thickness of one inch. The 33-foot hull should have a hull side thickness of at least 0.33 inches, a bottom thickness of 0.66 inches and a keel thickness of 1.25 inches. The thickness of the bottom and keel may need to be increased if the boat speed is over 30 knots or if there are two heavy engines.

WORKING DRAWINGS
FOR YOUR BOAT

Whether you buy a hull or build it, you will need drawings to show the location of the engines, bulkheads and all the interior. Often, a person who sells a bare hull will have scale drawings of boats that have been previously built from that hull. If you talk with one of these owners, ask what arrangement they used, what power produced what boat speed, what problems they had and if the boat floated level when launched. Any changes you make from the drawings may seriously affect the trim of the completed boat. The center of the underwater hull volume (center of buoyancy) should be marked on the drawings. The total center of gravity of everything in the boat must be at the fore-and-aft location of the center of buoyancy if the boat is to float in a level position.

There are a few companies and many boat designers that sell stock plans for every type of boat. These plans are usually available at a small fraction of the cost of a custom design and listed in the classified ads of the boating magazines that discuss owner built boats. One source is "The Complete Guide To Boat Kits & Plans," P. O. Box 420235, Palm Coast FL 32142 - 0235.

These plans may be $200, where a custom design for a 25 or 33-foot boat would certainly have a fee of $4000 to $7000. Buy the catalogs or list of plans and then decide if a set of plans are available for a boat you might want. If you can't find drawings that are suitable, make a detailed list of your requirements to send them to a designer for his recommendations. Take your time with these contacts and the investigation of what is available in the market. Your initial decisions will be followed by a large investment in time and money for a boat you will use for many years.

The following is the minimum number of drawings that should be provided (See Figure 1):

Hull and Deck Lines
Construction Plan & Profile
Table of Offsets
Construction Sections
Boat Profile
Engine & Shaft Installation
Interior Arrangement
Sail Plan & Ballast Drawing

Each drawing should show exactly which material is used, what thickness is specified and how it is secured in the hull. Every detail should be carefully read so there is complete understanding of how each part of the boat is built. Any questions should be explained by the designer or seller of the bare hull. Don't start construction until you understand every detail on the drawings.

I assume you have selected the drawings for a boat with some eating and sleeping accommodations that provide minimum facilities for two people. If you have chosen an open boat without any creature comforts, the previously mentioned costs and labor hours will be substantially reduced. Whatever you select, the construction process is just about the same for any glass fiber boat of any length.

SUMMARY

When you build your boat you get your custom arrangement exactly as you want it, without any compromises. You also know every detail of construction and are assured the boat is built to very high standards. Together with the satisfaction of a job well done, there are many reasons for building your boat, your way.

Summarizing the main points of this chapter, you first select the type of boat you want and the length you can afford. This decision is usually made by the construction costs and the cost of obtaining building facilities. Secondly, you obtain a set of drawings from a qualified designer or locate a bare hull. You are then ready to proceed with the construction process.

There are two methods of building a custom glass hull and each will be described. Laminating over a male plug is described in Chapters Two through Four, and laminating inside a female mold is described in a later chapter. Both methods are about the same cost, but the female mold method allows using the mold for many more identical hulls without requiring the tedious sanding of the outside of the hull. However, the female mold method does require more detailed building of the mold and fitting of the mold panels on which the hull will be laminated.

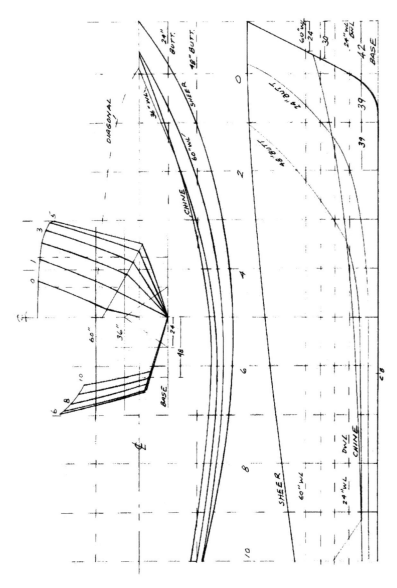

Figure 1

Hull lines drawing for a planing hull.

CHAPTER TWO
MALE PLUG LOFTING
& FRAMEWORK

You certainly will not have a problem understanding the interior construction drawings, but the hull and deck lines may seem strange to those who are not familiar with boat building. These drawings will be explained. Also, you may not be familiar with the male plug or the building of the construction framework on which the glass will be laminated, unless the drawings that you purchased were specifically intended for building by the owner. For these reasons, we will discuss the procedure for the glass lamination of a custom hull over a wood plug.

The shape of the hull is determined by the shape of the plug on which the hull is laminated, and the transverse (port to starboard) frames in the plug must be cut exactly to the hull shape, less the thickness of the glass laminate. The hull lines (Figure 1) are normally drawn to the outside of the hull for wood or glass fiber hulls, and conversely for steel and aluminum hulls. The plug will be similar to that in Figure 2 although powerboats will normally have a V-bottom shape instead of round.

LOFTING

The drawing of the hull lines (Figure 1) will have to be exactly reproduced on the floor to full size in order to obtain the frame shape for the plug. This is called "lofting" from the custom of olden times when the attic or "loft" over the boat building shop was used to draw the full size hull lines. Patterns for the deck shape are also taken from the loft.

A wood floor is ideal for lofting, but plywood panels over a rough concrete surface work just as well if the panels are secured to form a smooth area on which to work. A two inch square batten about ten feet longer than the boat is a necessity for drawing the lines. Smaller, half-inch square by ten-foot battens are used for the shape of the transverse sections. Lead or steel window sash weights or similar weights are used by the dozen to hold the battens in the desired position.

The hull lines are reproduced exactly as shown on the small scale drawings with a profile, plan view and sections. An accurate grid is drawn first, consisting of straight lines for the baseline, horizontal waterlines in profile, and section and vertical station (section) lines in plan and profile. The curved shape of the sections (body plan) are taken from the measurements (Offsets) on the plan and profile views at each vertical station line. (See Figure 1)

Drawing of the curved lines is accomplished by plotting all the points given in the Table of Offsets you received with your drawings. The long batten is then placed on these points and a pencil line drawn through them. The batten is held in place with weights or temporary nails. The batten may have to be repositioned two or three times to get a smooth, fair line between all the plotted points. The weights are always placed on the inside of the curve. If one or two points are not on the edge of the batten, but the rest of the points are in position, go ahead and draw the line and make a note of the errors on the Table of Offsets. A good set of hull lines will not have errors or oversights of more than one-eighth of an inch, which is very hard to see when the designer is working with a scale of 3/4" = 1' 0(1:16).

Figure 2

Male plug for a sailboat. The hull will be laminated on this form.

The lofting may seem a strange and boring process, but the necessity of having accurate patterns of the hull shape becomes evident when you build and fair the male plug. The shape of the deck is also drawn in all three views so patterns can be made for the shape of the tops of the bulkheads where they meet the deck. The position of each bulkhead is drawn on the loft, parallel to the vertical station lines, at the correct distance from the stem and stern. Patterns for each bulkhead can then be made. As you draw the hull lines full size, keep in mind the relationship of all three views and all dimensions must agree in all three views.

TEMPLATES

When the sections (body plan) are completed, make templates from wood, Mylar or cardboard for each station (usually ten) and for the transom. These templates are made by reproducing the loft dimensions directly on the template material or by placing the material over the loft and cuffing away until the outside hull shape is exactly reproduced. Mark the boat centerline and one or two waterlines that are common to all stations. If the template is glued together from more than one piece of material, use doublers to reinforce the seams and vertical pieces to be certain the template will remain in alignment. Only one side of the boat is necessary for a template as it can be turned over to get both port and starboard sides.

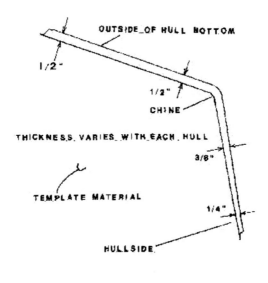

Figure 3

Measuring hull thickness on a hull station mold template.

Since the frames (station molds) represent the inside of the hull and the hull lines are drawn to the outside of the hull, the templates are then measured and cut away to the hull

34

thickness at that particular location on the hull. Remember the hull thickness varies throughout the hull. This hull thickness is taken from the drawings and measured perpendicular to the outside edge of the template or, more precisely, perpendicular to a tangent to the outside edge. (See Figure 3).

If the hull thickness is noted on the drawings in layers (plies) of laminate and not in inches of thickness, you will have to interpolate. The laminations usually consist of alternating layers of 1.5-ounce/sq-ft glass Mat and 19-ounce/sq-yd glass Woven Roving material. One ply of each is called a pair. It is only custom that weighs one material in square feet and the other in square yards. Each ply of Mat is about .050 inches in thickness when saturated with resin, and each ply of Woven Roving is about .040 inches thick when cured. The Mat absorbs more resin and is thus thicker in a completed laminate form.

If a core material is used in the hull sides, its thickness will also be subtracted from the outside of the template along with only the OUTSIDE laminate thickness. A core material is not recommended in the hull bottom as it may fail when the boat is pounded when on a trailer, or when the boat is set on only two keel blocks in a boatyard. Solid glass laminate must be used in the area of through hull fittings, rudder post and at the shaft struts.

FRAMES FOR THE MALE PLUG METHOD (STATION MOLDS)

The frames for the plug (station molds) are made from 1/2 or 3/4 thick plywood or from 1 x 12 straight wood planks. If more than one piece of material is used, the joints are covered with a doubler piece that is glued and screwed The boat centerline and one or two waterlines are marked on the frame material. An athwart ships 2 x 6 brace is screwed to the frame exactly so the top edge (toward the floor when upside down on the plug framework) is on the selected, level, waterline that is common to all frames (station molds). This edge will be set on the framework to align all frames.

When the template is aligned on the frame material and a curved scribe line is made on the outside edge, be certain that the centerline is accurately placed and that the port and starboard sides are identical. Be certain each waterline half distance is exact when measured from the boat centerline. Any error will be obvious when a batten is used to check the accuracy of all the frames after positioning on the framework.

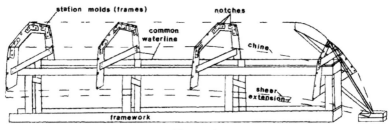

Figure 4

Male plug frame work

The frames must now be aligned to each other and strongly braced to support the weight of the completed hull. (See Figure 4) The frames are bolted to a rectangular 2 x 6 wood framework with steel angles. The framework extends from the transom to station zero and must be rigid, level and bolted to the floor with steel angles. The top edge of the rectangular framework is level and represents the selected, common waterline marked on all frames (station molds). The frames are set upside down on the framework to make it easier to laminate the glass and resin. The height of the rectangular wood framework must be sufficient so the bow and stern clear the floor when the selected common waterline is level. On the framework, mark the position of the AFT side of each forward frame and the FORWARD side of each aft frame to coincide with the station position on the drawings. The reason for this will become apparent when the frames are faired and the notches cut into them. Hold the long batten (it takes two people) on the edges of all the frames. If the batten is not touching every frame, check the alignment of the suspect frame. Bevel the edge of each forward frame with a power plane only on the forward portion of the frame edge. Bevel the edges of the aft frames only on the aft portion of the frame edges. The batten must touch each frame edge. Move the batten port and starboard to check the fairness at all portions of the frames.

Be certain each frame is bolted to the framework with steel angles, is aligned exactly to the station spacing, is exactly vertical and exactly on the boat centerline. Notches, spaced nine inches apart, are cut into the frame edges in order to fit 1 x 2 longitudinal wood battens. They will be more closely spaced in the bow areas. The bottom of each notch will be tapered to fit the batten as it bends toward the bow or stern. The battens must lie fair at each frame. If they do not fit the notch in the frame without forcing, the frame is not correct. When these longitudinal battens have been screwed to each frame (station mold), again use the long batten to check the fairness of all the frames.

THE DECK TO HULL JOINT

It may seem out of place, but now is the time to decide the configuration of the joint where the deck is attached to the hull. When you laminate the top edge of the hull (sheer), the glass has a tendency to become separated unless it is rolled into a strong, flat surface. Therefore, you must have an extension at the sheer in the form of a wood plank, either in line with or perpendicular to the top edge of the hull side (See Figure 5). The joint configuration shows whether or not an outward turning flange is required. This is shown in Figure 2 as the flat plank extending outward and perpendicular to the hull side at the sheer. The selection of the type of configuration is a matter of preference and where you want to place the rub rail.

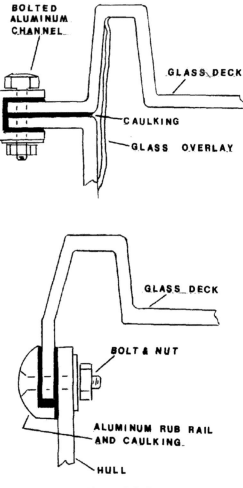

Figure 5 & 5a

Attaching the hull to the deck

A few boats have been built with a curve at the sheer so the deck curves into the hull side and no sharp line defines the sheer. This calls for some fine craftsmanship in finishing the outside surface and the placement of the rub rail well below the deck level. The inside of the hull must be reinforced with three pair of glass material where the deck is faired into the hull side.

Whatever joint configuration you choose, it will have to be carefully considered during the construction of the framework and the male plug.

SUMMARY

This chapter reviewed the building of the framework (plug) on which the hull will be laminated. In order to get frame patterns, the lines of the hull and deck are drawn full size on the loft. Extreme care must be taken at every stage of lofting, making templates and cutting frames (station molds). Setting the frames on the construction framework must be complete to precise standards. After fairing of the mold frames and the installation of the longitudinal battens, we are now ready to begin the hull laminations over the male plug.

At this point, let's review what has been accomplished and what will be done to complete the custom glass hull from a male plug:

1. Decide on the type of boat you want, try to locate a bare hull that fits your requirements or obtain suitable drawings.

2. Review the cost of building the boat and decide on the number and type of engines.

3. Obtain a suitable building with a door of suitable height and width. Alternately, a pipe frame and plastic covering may be used in the proper location and in fair weather.

4. Loft the hull and deck lines to obtain frame patterns if you are going to build a hull rather than buy a bare hull.

5. Build the mold frames and construction framework (male plug).

6. Decide on the attachment of the deck to the hull.

7. Install longitudinal battens to connect the mold frames, then cover the plug with plastic film to keep the hull from sticking.

8. Laminate glass on the plug to the desired thickness.

9. Use a long batten to check the fairness as you proceed.

10. Fill and sand the low areas to an acceptable smoothness.

11. Again check the fairing with a long batten and apply a paint finish.

CHAPTER THREE
LAMINATING THE HULL ON A MALE PLUG

The purpose of the longitudinal battens on the station mold framework is to stiffen the plug structure and to support the glass laminations. To prevent the wood from adhering to the glass, it is necessary to place a vinyl film, Mylar or cellophane, directly on the longitudinal battens with two-sided adhesive tape. Don't leave wrinkles in the film or they will be faithfully reproduced in the laminate.

BUYING THE GLASS MATERIAL

It is assumed you will use the least expensive materials, but I don't want to exclude any new developments or preferences each owner may have. Polyester resin is about one-quarter the cost of epoxy resin but it does have a strong odor of styrene that may not be tolerated by some people. Epoxy resin usually provides a stronger chemical bond and thus a stronger laminate if the cost is affordable. Resin has a shelf life of about three months and this should be checked with the supplier.

There are many types of glass material on the market, each with different knits or weaves and most with a higher cost than the ordinary mat and woven roving. It is probably best for most applications to stay with these minimum cost materials. The more expensive materials provide adequate strength in the laminate with lighter weight, but only very high speed boats need to reduce weight in the laminations. Whatever type of material is purchased, it must be kept in a cool, dry location. High humidity will reduce the strength of the chemical bond of the glass and resin.

It is difficult to estimate the amount of glass and resin required for the hull and for the entire boat, but we can roughly estimate that the deck will require the same amount of laminate as the hull, including overlays on the inside and local reinforcements. A usual laminate contains about 30 percent glass and 70 percent resin. The bare hull weight for a 25-foot hull is about 1200 pounds and a 33-foot hull would weigh about 3000 pounds. Therefore, a 25-foot hull would require about 360 pounds of glass and 840 pounds of resin. Allow ten percent for waste and spillage. Always apply laminate to meet the designer's specifications as a minimum. Do not try to scrimp on the laminate

PRELIMINARY PLANNING PRIOR TO LAMINATING

Plan the laminating by calculating the amount of 1.5-ounce mat and 19-ounce woven roving that will be required. If the total glass thickness in one area is one inch, use alternating layers of eleven plies of mat and eleven plies of woven roving. One of each material is called a pair and is about .090 inches in finished thickness. If a half-inch thickness is required, six pair should be used.

Lay one layer of dry woven roving on top of the plug to see whether the glass material fits better athwart ships or at an angle to the boat's centerline. After this trial fit, cut the mat and woven roving to an approximate length, leaving at least a foot extra at each sheer. Keep in mind that the first pair will be shorter than the last pair as the girth will increase as the laminate is applied. The edges of each piece of material will overlap another by at least two inches. Stagger this edge overlap on each pair of mat and woven roving to prevent a thickness buildup and the resulting unfair shape. Set aside the cut pairs of glass material in order of placement on the hull so there will be no interruption of lamination to find what piece of glass material goes at what location.

The entire lamination will not be completed in one day and you must take precautions that a good chemical bond will occur when the laminating is resumed. You can assure this by rolling on a layer of peel ply (Veil cloth), without any additional resin, when you have stopped the normal laminations. This and all rolling of laminate is done with a stainless steel disc roller. The lightweight peel ply material is available through your normal supplier and is literally peeled off and discarded when you are ready to proceed with the hull laminating.

APPLYING THE GLASS ON A MALE PLUG

If a core is used on the hull sides, it is placed on the plug with two sided adhesive tape and saturated with resin on the outside. The resin is applied with a disposable brush or roller. A layer of mat only is placed on the core material, resin is applied and is thoroughly rolled out with the stainless steel disc roller. The edges are overlapped and the mat is continued over the ending of the core at the designed waterline.

If no core material is used, a layer of 1 .5-ounce mat is laid dry on the plastic film and the edges are overlapped at least two inches. This mat is then wet with resin and one ply of woven roving is applied. Wet this roving with resin and roll thoroughly to remove any entrapped air and to squeeze any excess resin to the top. The ideal method of laminating is to wet the glass material with resin just enough to be saturated and to provide a good chemical bond between the glass fibers, but any excess resin should be avoided. Remember, the strength of the laminate is in the glass fibers and not in the resin.

If a core material is used, you will be laminating only the outside required amount of glass material. After the outside is finished and sanded, the inner laminate is applied when the hull is removed from the male plug. With or without a core, apply alternate layers of 1 .5-ounce mat and 19-ounce woven roving to the desired thickness, overlapping the edges and rolling each layer. This must be done with careful attention to detail. Any entrapped air will surely lead to delamination.

You have previously trimmed the station molds to compensate for the variations in hull thickness, so the concentration must now be on getting the laminations as smooth as possible, without any humps or hollows. It doesn't matter whether the additional laminations for the bottom and keel areas are applied first or last, but you must adhere to the amount and location where the station molds were trimmed.

After applying two or three pair of glass material, look for areas of humps and hollows, checking with the long batten. The low spots can be identified with colored chalk and then outlined with temporary strips of tape. Move the long batten over the entire hull surface. Apply a mixture of filler (micro balloons) and resin to these low spots and lightly sand them with a coarse grit to match the surrounding high spots. Do not sand on the glass material; sand only on the filler. Again use the long batten to check the progress. Fill, sand and proceed with the laminate.

SANDING THE HULL ON A MALE PLUG

Sanding is a long and tedious process and one that can be grossly abused if the sanding is done in the wrong areas with the wrong method.

The sanding is only done on the filler of micro balloons and resin. The long batten is constantly used to show what areas require fairing. If you want a perfect hull surface that will look great with a high gloss finish, there is no substitute for many hours of sanding.

A small disc sander usually leaves a series of flat spots or grooves and is not suitable for hull fairing. There are patented, slow speed disc sanders on the market with a large diameter pad and they are a great improvement. Probably the most efficient at minimum cost is a long sanding board used by two people. This board is foam covered and about six feet long and nine inches wide. Adhesive is used to affix sandpaper to the foam and two people push the board over the filled high spots in order to achieve fairness.

When you are satisfied with the smoothness of the hull, apply a primer and paint strictly in accordance with the manufacturer's instructions. There are many fine finishes on the market specifically designated for glass fiber hulls. Do not scrimp on the primers recommended as you must have a completely waterproof barrier to prevent water from reaching the glass laminate. If you do not have spray equipment, be sure to select a finish that can be applied by roller. If you do have spray equipment, be certain to apply the correct thickness of the primer and the finish coat.

The drawing of the hull lines should show the estimated waterline (designed waterline) at which the boat will float. This waterline can be scribed into the paint (not the glass hull) as it is drying. Reference points on the hull lines drawing can be used to fix the waterline at the bow, stern and amidships. These points may be connected by using the long batten or by using water-filled clear plastic tubing. The latter is accomplished by using clear plastic tubing of any diameter and about ten feet longer than the boat. One end of the tubing is held near the bow mark for the waterline so that the water level in the tubing is exactly on this mark. The water level in the other end of the tubing shows the same level and is moved to any point on the hull to scribe the waterline. This method assumes the boat is sitting level with the designed water line. The anti-fouling bottom paint should be applied to a point one or two inches above this scribed waterline. If a decorative boot top is painted with a contrasting color, the anti-fouling is applied up to the bottom of the boot top. If there is some question about where the boat will float, many apply the boot top after launching.

CHAPTER FOUR
TURNING THE HULL UPRIGHT

THE CRADLE FOR THE HULL

The hull needs a cradle in which to sit while the interior and deck are built (See Figure 6, Parts 1 through 4) and it is best to build this cradle on the hull while it is upside down on the male plug. Three-quarter inch plywood is used for these cradle outside frames with the inside shape cut to the hull shape. This inside curved edge is made softer by gluing scrap carpet material to the plywood edge. Seams of the plywood are connected with 1 x 12 wood doublers, bolted to both pieces. The tops of the cradle frames have a two-inch projection on each side to hold the hull in the cradle while it is turned. The extreme top of the cradle frames will sit on the floor. There are three or more cradle frames spaced six to eight feet apart, depending on the hull length. These cradle frames are connected on the bottom with two 2 x 6 longitudinals. These longitudinals also have carpet on the top edge and are bolted to the cradle frames with 1 x 4 steel angles.

The 45-degree flat portions on the bottom of the cradle must be in the same plane on all the cradle frames. This can be checked with the long batten. Each 45-degree flat should be at least three feet in length and the total width of each cradle frame is about six feet wider than the beam of the boat, at the maximum point. Each frame must have the same width. It is

47

important to build the cradle strongly and accurately. It will be a permanent structure to use for winter storage during the life of the hull and when the boat is hauled for repairs.

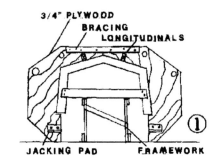

3/4" PLYWOOD
BRACING
LONGITUDINALS

JACKING PAD   FRAMEWORK   ①

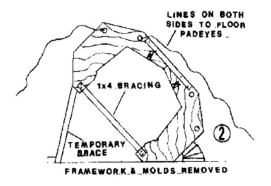

LINES ON BOTH
SIDES TO FLOOR
PADEYES

1x4 BRACING

TEMPORARY
BRACE   ②

FRAMEWORK & MOLDS REMOVED

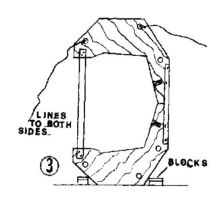

LINES
TO BOTH
SIDES

③   BLOCKS

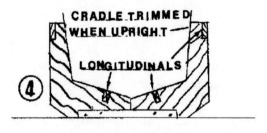

Figure 6 parts 1-4

Turning the hull with a cradle.

When the cradle is installed on the outside of the hull and connected with longitudinals, the construction framework and hull station molds can be removed from inside the hull. Actually, they can be removed later, but it may be easier to unbolt the framework while the hull is upside down, rather than stand in the hull and lift the wood over the sheer. On the other hand, if you plan to use the male plug for other hulls, the structure remains inside the hull until it is upright, when it is removed by crane. If you do remove the structure at this point, it may be easier to unbolt the mold frames first as they will be partially supported by the framework and will not fall on you.

ROTATING THE MALE PLUG

There are three methods of turning the hull upright.

1. Use a crane inside or outside the building. In the latter case, the hull and framework will have to be moved outside on casters.

2. Use a block and tackle hanging from structural roof supports, if they are of sufficient strength.

3. Use jacks, blocks and lines on both sides to slowly rotate the hull.

The expected loads must be carefully considered. The

25-foot glass hull will be about 1200 pounds, the cradle about 900 pounds and the building framework about 600 pounds, for a total of 2700 pounds. The 33-foot hull is about 3000 pounds and with the cradle and framework would weigh about 4800 pounds. The cradle and framework can be weighed on scales after assembly or piece by piece.

Rotating the hull to an upright position must be done slowly and safely. You must have control over the hull movement at all times. This means if you pull the cradle in one direction, there must be a restraining line in the opposite direction. If you install casters on the cradle to roll it outside, each caster should have a load limit equal to the weight of the completed boat as these casters are permanent fixtures.

When a crane is used to turn the hull, it is an easy matter to attach the crane to the middle of the cradle assembly and pull it to the next flat spot on the cradle bottom. The important point is to brace and block the cradle at each step, before the crane is detached. The weight of one person climbing on the cradle to detach the crane hook may change the center of gravity to the point of instability. Always use blocks and bracing to prevent movement.

When there is no lifting equipment available, there must be strong anchor points (padeyes or screw eyes) to tie off the pulling and restraining lines that are on each cradle frame. See Figure 6. These padeyes can be put into a concrete floor with epoxy glue in two inch deep holes. The turning force is provided by hydraulic jacks working against steel angles bolted to the cradle. Jack the cradle up to the limit of the jacks and install blocks at all parts of the cradle.

This jacking process is continued by repositioning them on blocks to enable tilting the cradle again until it is on a 45-degree flat. Blocks are positioned on the low side of the cradle to prevent any unwanted further movement. This procedure is continued until the hull is upright in the cradle. The excess plywood is then cut from the sides of the cradle and two more longitudinals are installed near the sheer. The height of the cradle may then be about 12 inches below the sheer so it will not interfere with the attachment of the deck. Use blocks to level the hull so the interior may be installed level and plumb. Do not assume the floor or cradle is level. It is the hull that must be level and the scribed waterline may be used as a reference line.

CHAPTER FIVE
BUILDING THE HULL IN A FEMALE MOLD

This method of building a mold in which to laminate the glass hull uses plywood or a sheet of plastic laminate as a mold surface. This is usually not as glossy as a permanent manufacture's mold and will only last for the laminating of a few hulls, where a production mold may last for 120 hulls. But we are talking about custom hulls and this female mold method provides a large saving in time as the outside of the hull will require little, if any, sanding.

When you purchase a set of drawings for use with this method of molding, it is most efficient to have the hull lines "conically developed" or simply called "developed lines". This means the hull shape will accept a sheet of material that cannot be bent into compound curves without cutting or creasing. When seen in the section view, all the lines are convex and do not have flare to the forward sections. This still produces an efficient hull shape. You don't want too fine a point on it, but a sheet of material can only be curved into a cylinder or a cone. To achieve other shapes the material must be cut or creased.

Of course, the glass can be molded into any shape, but here we are talking about building the female mold surface. If we have compound curves in the hull shape, the mold surface will have to be made from small, triangular pieces as in the making of a globe or a dome building. It is much easier and faster to have the hull lines computer generated with fully developed lines.

FRAMES FOR THE FEMALE MOLD

After selecting the type of boat you want and purchasing the drawings, the hull lines must be drawn full size (lofting) to obtain frame patterns. The plywood frames are set on longitudinals and serve to support the mold surface and the laminating of the glass hull (See Figure 7). Review the Chapter Two section on lofting hull lines and taking frame patterns.

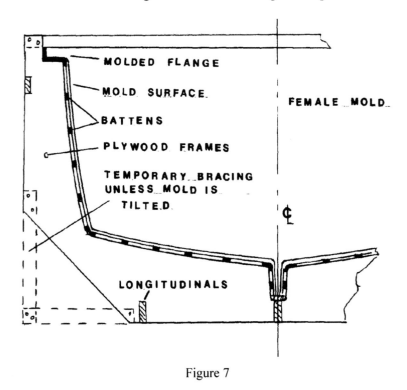

MOLDED FLANGE

MOLD SURFACE

BATTENS

PLYWOOD FRAMES

TEMPORARY BRACING
UNLESS MOLD IS
TILTED

FEMALE MOLD

LONGITUDINALS

Figure 7

Female mold construction showing plywood frames, battens and a high gloss interior surface.

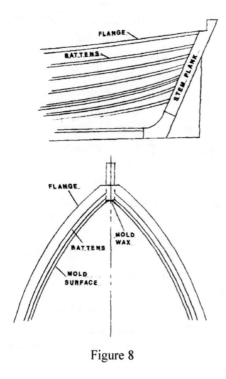

Figure 8

Female mold bow construction.

The outside frames for this female mold are made from three-quarter inch plywood with the seams reinforced with I x 12 planks. The inboard edge represents the outside surface of the hull, less the thickness of the mold surface and the longitudinal battens. This thickness is subtracted from the frame patterns perpendicular to the mold surface. The hull lines drawing is usually made to the outside of the hull surface which is the inside of the mold surface. For example, if the mold battens are actually three-quarter by one and one-half inch, laid on the flat (not edgewise) and the mold surface is half inch plywood plus sealers and paint, one and five-sixteenths inches will have to be subtracted from the frame patterns, (added to the hull lines) over the entire surface.

The frames are cut to the stations (sections) on the hull lines, of which there are usually ten, spaced equally on the waterline length of the hull. On a 33-foot hull, the waterline length might be 27.5 feet and the stations and mold frames are 2.75 feet (33 inches) apart. On longer hulls the female mold frames should not be more than 42 inches apart, in order to give sufficient support to the mold surface. For example, if the hull lines station spacing is 48 inches on a 40-foot waterline length hull, twenty stations should be drawn on the hull lines and loft so the female mold frames are 24 inches apart.

The keel is built into the frames with a mold surface just as on the rest of the hull. From the hull lines and loft, a wood 2 x 6 stem and keel support is cut to the necessary shape, to fit outside the actual dimensions. These are supported by the 2 x 6 longitudinals on the bottom of the female mold. Since the keel bottom and the stem are tapered and curved in shape, the 2 x 6 wood plank supports will have to be built up from the bottom of the hull female mold.

Each mold frame should have temporary, horizontal 2 x 4 braces at the top. The boat centerline should be carefully marked. The top of the frames should extend about 12 inches above the sheer line to give extra room for laminating and rolling to make sure the laminate is flat at the sheer, but only if a horizontal flange is not required for the joint of the deck to the hull. If you do want a flange extending outboard, it must be installed after the frames are set vertically.

From the hull lines and loft, mark the station locations on the 2 x 6 bottom longitudinals. Because of the curvature of the hull shape, set the forward frames with the AFT edge of the frame exactly on the station marks. Set the aft frames with the FORWARD edge on the station mark. This will leave the battens resting only on one edge of the frames but it does eliminate the necessity for beveling each frame. You can use glued wood wedges or polyester resin putty to fill the gaps between batten and frame. Be certain each frame is accurately placed on the station spacing. This placement determines the entire hull shape.

BATTENS & THE FEMALE MOLD SURFACE

Many wood battens support the mold surface and can have actual dimensions of three-quarter inch by one and one-half inches or larger. These are located about nine inches apart throughout the hull and keel and are nailed or screwed to the mold frames, with recessed fastener heads, after the mold frames have been erected, braced and faired.

Use temporary bracing to set each mold frame vertically on the 2 x 6 bottom longitudinals The boat centerline must be exactly aligned and each side of the hull frames must be exactly the same distance from the centerline. Use 4 x 4 steel angles to secure the frames to the longitudinals. Use the long batten to check the inside of the frames and trim or reposition them as necessary. Each frame must be exactly fair. Check and recheck until each frame has an accurate shape and is the same on both sides.

The battens will have to be scarfed to get sufficient material for the boat length, which should be done with epoxy glue over a twelve-inch length. Use select wood to avoid knots and checks. These battens will be closely spaced at the stem and will stiffen the entire structure.

The mold surface is glued to the battens and is cut to fit exactly in all areas of the hull. The material may be painted plywood, plywood covered with a plastic laminate or sheets of solid plastic. The objective of the mold surface is to have all the seams perfectly filled so the defect is not transferred to the hull and to have a very glossy finish so the hull will be the same.

The least expensive material to use is exterior grade plywood with many coats of filler and paint on the inside. The outside of the plywood can be glassed to the outside of the battens with small pieces of glass mat. The outside of the plywood can be coated with resin at the same time. This avoids any moisture absorption. Half-inch thick plywood is the thickest that can be pushed into the hull shape without using heavy weights or block and tackle on the outside. One quarter-inch thick plywood can also be used, with caution.

If you purchase hull lines that have been developed by computer, you may also be able to purchase the "shell development" or actual dimensions of the hull panels in the flat, uncurved, position. If not, you must make patterns from heavy paper, cardboard or other material made specifically for patterns. Lay the pattern material on the battens, exactly on centerline and scribe the chine line, making sure the pattern is lying tightly on the battens. Do the same between chine and sheer for the full length of the hull. Do not walk on the battens but on a sheet of plywood, carefully. It may be more convenient to build a scaffold across the mold with a lower level fitting inside the mold.

The mold surface material is then cut from the patterns and glued to the battens, using sandbags or weights to hold the panels in position. Double check all panels for an exact fit before gluing. Trim the panels so the butt seams are almost invisible. Plastic filler may be used to fill any cavities and blemishes. Be certain each square inch of the mold surface is perfect, as any blemish will be faithfully transferred to the glass hull. At least a half-inch radius is desired at the chine, keel and a two inch radius at the stem. These can be made with mold wax and fillers. Bare plywood is then filled, lightly sanded and painted with a glossy paint compatible with the styrene in the polyester laminating resin. Four coats should suffice. These and plastic sheets are then coated with wax and a mold releasing film.

LAMINATING THE HULL
IN A FEMALE MOLD

There are some important differences in laminating a glass hull in a female mold instead of over a male plug, but the basic glass material, resin and methods are the same. It is recommended that you review the laminating procedures as outlined in Chapter Three. Access to the mold is via the scaffolding you have built, or by tilting the framework to a 45 degree position. If the mold is tilted, blocks must be used on the opposite side to keep the whole structure stable.

After the mold has been waxed and a mold release film applied, you can apply the gel coat with a roller or spray equipment. The gel coat can be purchased from the glass and resin supplier in various colors and for different applications. If you spray the gel coat, be certain it is applied evenly and with at least a .020 inch thickness. Water absorption through the gel coat has occurred in many hulls where the gel coat was too thin, probably caused when the spray was moved too quickly over the hull surface. Be very cautious with this coating as it is the vital link in keeping water away from the glass laminate.

A layer of mat is laid against the gel coat and thoroughly wet and rolled to removed any air pockets. Take ample time and care with this first layer of mat. Proceed with another mat against the mat, wet, roll and continue with alternating layers of mat and woven roving until the required thickness is attained. Additional required laminate in the keel, at the chine, hull bottom, stem and transom is then added. Overlap the edges of all pairs at least two inches but stagger these overlaps in succeeding layers of laminate. The reinforcing glass at the keel and chine should overlap about twelve inches.

If a core material is desired in the hull sides, the top and bottom edges must be tapered about four inches to allow for a smooth transition to the solid laminate. The laminate where the deck is attached to the hull must be of solid glass. After the required thickness of solid laminate has been laid on the hull sides to meet the OUTSIDE laminate thickness of the core construction, the core is wet with resin and laid against the wet laminate. The laminations then continue, but using only the inside laminate thickness required over the core. Make sure the butt edges of the core material are wet with resin and fit tightly, without gaps.

After the laminate is completed, the bulkheads will be installed as explained in the next chapter. This can be completed before the hull is lifted from the female mold or after the hull is set in a cradle. Sometimes, the entire hull and deck are completed while still resting in the female mold, assuming the mold is not needed for another hull. Cradle construction is described in Chapter Four, but in this case, the cradle shape is determined from the loft dimensions rather than from templating the hull itself and the hull is lifted into the cradle.

Lifting the hull from the female mold is accomplished with a crane -- or other lift -- attached to two glass straps. These two straps are glassed to the inside of the hull about six feet from the bow and stern. Four straps may be preferable with boats over 35 feet in length. In the event the transom slopes forward from bottom to deck, there must be a removable, bolted transom section on both the male plug and on the female mold. This is called a "loose piece" in foundry terminology. The seams are filled and rounded with mold putty before applying the mold release film for each hull.

CHAPTER SIX
INSTALLING THE BULKHEADS

In order to maintain the hull shape during construction, the bulkheads should be installed as the next step. They must be vertical, in the correct location and must not fit tightly to the hull. The fore-and-aft location of the bulkheads is taken from the drawings after measuring the length of the hull to see if it is the same as indicated on the drawings. If there is a discrepancy, any shortfall can be taken in the lazarette or the forepeak. If the hull is longer than intended, add the length where the accommodations are the most crowded.

If the bulkheads are fit tightly to the hull, the edges will produce an unsightly line on the outside of the hull. To prevent this, the bulkhead does not reach the hull but is set on a foam and glass transverse frame with glass overlay, or it has glass overlay with resin putty at the edges. See Figure 9 which shows the two suggestions.

Use glass overlay of two mat alternating with two woven roving to attach the bulkheads to the hull and to other wood assemblies. This is called "secondary bonding" and refers to any glass laminate applied to the inside of the hull after the hull has been laminated. The problem is obtaining a good chemical bond with the cured laminate of the hull. The solution is to have a clean, sanded, dry hull inside surface. The attaching bond will be severely reduced if the glass hull or wood is dirty, oily, wet with condensation or covered with glass or wood dust. Use a sander with a coarse grit for 12 inches each side of the bulkhead where the glass will be applied. Patience and cleanliness are key.

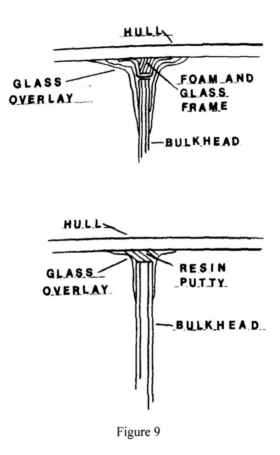

Figure 9

Two methods of attaching the bulkheads to the hull.

Marking the hull with the correct bulkhead location is always tedious as you must be very accurate. Be certain the location on the drawings is to the centerline of the bulkhead or forward or aft edge. Whatever is shown, continue with the same designation. After marking all locations on the hull centerline, check and recheck the dimensions so they add up to the actual length of the hull.

It is easiest to stretch a line from stem to transom at centerline. Use a tape measure from the stem and drop a plumb bob from the tape measure and boat centerline to the centerline at the keel. The boat must be level in order to use a plumb bob. If the hull has an open, box keel, put a strip of tape where the plumb bob hits centerline, with the tape secured to either side on the hull. In this manner, the bulkhead location can be marked on both sides of the keel.

If a straight 2 x 4 is placed across the sheer exactly at the bulkhead location, the hull can be marked at the sheers also, and a line scribed on the inside of the hull with a fine tipped felt pen (not with a grease pencil) from sheer to keel. If the boat has a chine, a board can be cut to fit across the chines and just resting on the plumb bob line. This establishes the bulkhead location at the chines. When these boards are used to mark the bulkhead location, measure from each end to the stem at centerline to make sure the board is exactly perpendicular to the boat centerline. This measurement is repeated when the final bulkhead is set.

CUTTING & GLASSING THE BULKHEADS

So far, you have marked the hull where the bulkheads are located. This is extremely important as you must have sufficient room between bulkheads to build the interior. The bulkheads are cut to templates made from cardboard, bristol board or scrap plywood. Be certain the edge is one or two inches inside the hull surface, depending on the method of attachment that you choose. (See Figure 9)

The bulkhead material can be half-inch exterior plywood on a 25-foot hull, five-eighths thick on a 33-foot hull and three-quarter inch thick in hulls forty feet to sixty feet in length. If you use pre-finished plywood with a plastic laminate or rare wood covering, you must cut this coating out to a width of four inches at the edges where the glass overlay will be applied. At this point, it may be wise to briefly discuss the material and finishing options for the bulkheads.

First of all, the least expensive wood finish is paint or colored resin. This is washable and gives a clean appearance. Secondly, you can apply plastic laminate of many colors and textures, with the inboard edge covered in the same plastic laminate. The outboard edges will have a curved wood trim piece. Thirdly, the bulkhead can be stained and varnished, but this requires some maintenance. Fourth, washable, textured vinyl coverings can be used with a wood or metal trim piece on both the inboard and outboard edges. Fifth, you can apply any type of rare wood or textured plastic that fits your decorative plan.

Be certain the tops of each bulkhead are cut to the exact shape of the underside of the deck or cabin top. This takes careful planning on the loft and some builders prefer to have the bulkhead top edges extend to a few inches above the deck or cabin top. They make the final cut when a long batten can be placed across all the bulkheads to insure a smooth, fair line throughout the length of the deck.

When you are sure the position of each bulkhead is marked correctly on the hull, you can install the glass over foam transverse frames. Position each bulkhead temporarily with braces to the hull and recheck the shape of the outboard edge and the distance to centerline of the inboard edge. Be certain the bulkhead is plumb and glassed to the hull with three mat alternating with woven roving. If resin putty is used on the hull to bed the bulkheads, place it on the scribed line and install the plywood bulkhead while the putty is soft, one at a time. Use temporary bracing to the hull and make sure the bulkhead is exactly vertical.

CHAPTER SEVEN
INSTALLING THE CABIN SOLE

After the bulkheads are installed, most builders install the cabin sole (flooring), as it gives a level platform on which to work. The material used may be exterior plywood coated with resin on both sides and painted with a nonskid coating on the top. Exterior plywood with a teak veneer is also very popular. Expensive boats vary from plywood covered with carpeting to plywood covered with a teak 1 x 2 lattice arrangement with square holes. The latter looks good but the holes collect dust and lint.

Both the hull and the cabin sole must be supported to prevent flexing. The sole is primarily supported by the engine girders (two or four) that run the length of the hull. These girders have a core of wood, solid glass fiber or foam. They are secured to the hull with four alternating layers of mat and woven roving, extending at least six inches over the hull surface. Other hull bottom and hull side stiffeners are shown on the drawings you have purchased. They are spaced 20 or 30 inches apart and secured in a similar manner. It is easiest to glass in these stiffeners while the hull is open. Careful study of the interior arrangement must be made so these stiffeners are placed where they do not interfere with usable space. For example, locate a stiffener to coincide with the underside of the galley and head counters, so the stiffener is used for support of the counter. Another example would be a glass stiffener which supports the underside of a berth, while the stiffener 20 inches above supports a shelf.

Cleats on the bulkheads support the cabin sole and the girders provide fore-and-aft support. The outboard edges of the sole must be glassed to the hull to form a watertight compartment. If the boat is to be made non-sinkable, install foam outboard of the girders in a space that would not otherwise be used. If a tank is to be installed under the sole, a cut may be made in the sole for possible tank removal and the seam hidden with an aluminum T-molding and caulking. Access to storage is made with commercially available hatches (such as Bomar 8812) that are flush with the sole and can be located anywhere, especially at through hull fittings, bilge pumps and valves on top of tanks.

Hatches can also be carefully cut into the cabin sole with the piece cut being used for the hatch itself An aluminum T-molding is screwed to the edge of the hatch to hide the seam. Wood 1 x 2 cleats are screwed under the edges of the sole to support the weight of a person standing on the hatch. Any large hatch -- and the entire cabin sole -- must be supported by the engine girders below, or vertical posts if the unsupported span is longer than 24 inches. These posts can be 2 x 2 wood, screwed to wood floor beams at the top, and glassed to hull framing at the bottom.

When the unsupported span is more than 24 inches, transverse 2 x 3 floor beams must be glued and screwed to the bottom of the cabin sole from port edge to starboard edge. For example, if the distance between bulkheads is 80 inches, the floor beams will be spaced 20 inches apart with each one having a vertical post both port and starboard, ten inches and then thirty inches off the centerline. The hull stiffeners, which also secure the bottom of the posts, are located longitudinally, parallel to the boat centerline and 20 to 30 inches apart, according to the drawings. These form the base support for the vertical posts which are glassed to them and support the sole.

CHAPTER EIGHT
TANKS

The installation of both fuel and water tanks and their piping is of prime importance as it is normally permanent and must be correct the first time. After the boat is completed, it is very difficult to remove the tanks or piping for any repairs. Not only must the fuel and water systems be watertight but they have to withstand vibration and impact loads that are transmitted by the hull.

Fuel, water and waste tanks may be of different materials but generally, fuel tanks are aluminum and water tanks are stainless steel. There are some plastic tanks on the market solely for water but some of these are not the best quality, because the pipe fittings are glued plastic rather than bronze. Separate tanks are used with glass fiber hulls as vibration can loosen the glass bond of tanks integral with the hull (where the hull is used as one side of the tank). Integral tanks may be used on steel or aluminum hulls.

TANK LOCATION

Tanks are often located in the bottom of the hull, directly on top of the longitudinal frames that support them. In this manner, the center of gravity is as low as possible. When there is insufficient space in the bilge for all the required fuel, the tanks are installed outboard against the side of the hull. These tanks may extend from the bilge to the deck in the engineroom, leaving a walkway between the engines. Often, the water tank is installed on centerline in the bilges, but supported by framing.

Tanks can be on centerline or on either side of the hull but must never extend across the boat from port to starboard. The latter condition allows the liquid to flow from side to side with each roll of the boat. This movement increases the amount of the roll and makes the boat uncomfortable if not dangerous. The baffles within the tanks do little to lessen this problem. If the entire bilge area of the hull is filled with tanks, do not use the top of the tank to support the cabin sole. Install floor beams over the tanks and use vertical posts between the edges of the tanks to support the cabin sole (See Figure 10).

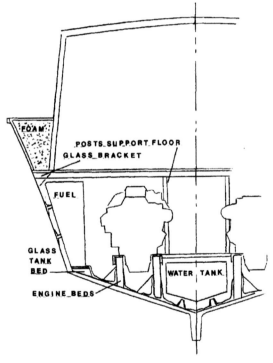

Figure 10

Section of a fiberglass powerboat showing the arrangement of the tanks in the engineroom.

The longitudinal location of all tanks should be close to the boat's center of gravity (usually slightly aft of the middle of the boat) so the trim of the boat is not affected when the tanks are completely full or empty. If the tanks are at the stern, the boat will be down by the stern when the tanks are full and down by the bow when the tanks are empty. Therefore the boat will run poorly even with high horsepower.

Diesel fuel is pumped by the engine fuel pump in much greater volume than is used by the injectors and most of this diesel fuel is returned to the tank. The temperature of this returned fuel is over 100 degrees. If the fuel tank is under a berth, the stateroom can become excessively warm, but insulation around the tank will correct this problem

One or more tanks are used for each engine so clean fuel can be delivered to any engine in case one tank is contaminated. Larger boats have two water tanks for the same reason. It is convenient to have a separate fuel tank for the AC generator, as it runs on a different time schedule than the engines. Otherwise, fuel will have to be pumped from one tank to another to even the fuel supply in the tanks.

A sketch of a diesel fuel piping system is shown in Figure 11. This diagram shows fuel can be taken from or returned to any tank. The fuel transfer pump is used to move fuel from one tank to another. The stop valves isolate one tank or one engine, from the others. The check valves insure that the flow in a pipe is only in the correct direction. These stop valves are located in the engineroom, grouped together in a "manifold".

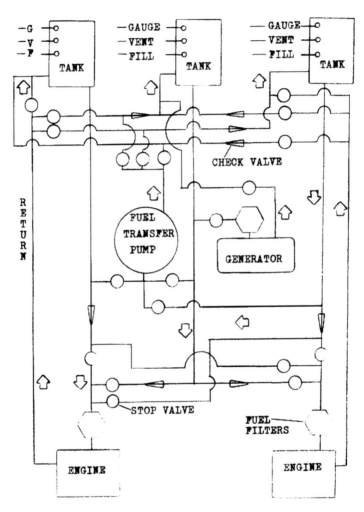

Figure 11

Diesel fuel piping system. In normal operation each engine would be supplied from one tank.

TANK THICKNESS

All tanks should be tested to 5 psi and built to the U.S. Coast Guard requirements for small passenger vessels (CG -323). Tanks in large hulls should be tested to a greater pressure if the fill or vent piping top is more than 11 feet from the bottom of the tank. This occurs when these pipes are full and exert a higher pressure on the tank. One foot of vertical piping exerts about 0.45 psi on the tank below.

All tanks must have baffles spaced not more than 20 inches apart to stiffen the tank sides and to prevent rapid flow of the liquid from one end to the other. Each baffle has a three-inch hole in the center and has the corners cut out. If the tank is more than three feet in height, there should be additional framing, either inside or outside the tank.

The thickness of the tank material may be calculated using a standard engineering formula for the thickness of beams supported by stiffeners on the ends. We use the test pressure of 5 psi or greater, a stiffener spacing of 20 inches and the allowable yield or bending strength of the tank material. An aluminum tank has a yield strength of 18,000 psi, while a steel tank is 30,000 psi. This example uses an aluminum tank:

$t^2 = P (S^2)$ divided by twice the yield strength
(t = thickness, P = pressure, 5 = spacing)
$t^2 = 5 (400)$ divided by $36000 = 0.0555$ and $t = .236$ inches thick.

On the top of each tank there should be a six-inch, threaded, watertight inspection plate for inspection and cleaning. There will be no fittings on the bottom or sides of the tank as a leak would flood the hull. A tank should always rest on, and be secured to, the framing but never directly on the hull.

CHAPTER NINE
THE ENGINEROOM

The type of engines and equipment used in the engineroom varies greatly. Figure 12 is only one representation of what an average boat may have on board. Probably the most important problem in the engineroom is securing the engines and all equipment so they will not become loose as a result of vibration and impact loads. The engines are secured to longitudinal girders spaced according to the engine mount spacing. If the forward and aft mount spacing is different, the girders are usually set at an average spacing. It is best to purchase the mounts from the engine manufacturer and proceed according to this final spacing. Steel brackets are custom fabricated to fit between the girder thickness and the bolting pattern of the engine mounts. The location of the steel brackets and height of the girders is templated from the engine with the mounts attached.

In a glass fiber hull it is best to have the engine girders made of solid glass in the engineroom even though the girders have a foam core forward and aft of the engineroom. In this manner, the steel engine brackets can be bolted through the sides of the girders. There is a great concentration of weight in the engineroom area and there should be extra transverse frames (webs) at half the normal spacing in the engineroom, and also under tanks if the tanks are in a separate space.

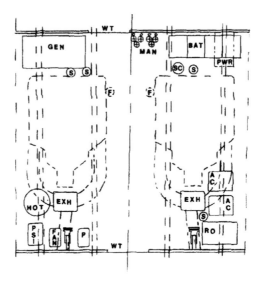

Figure 12

Engineroom plan: AC-Air Conditioning, BAT-Battery, EXH-Collector for engine exhaust, F-Fuel filters, FAN-Air exhaust fan, GEN-Genset, HOT-Hot water tank, MAN-Manifrid for fuel and water valves, P-Bilge pump, PSI-pressure water pump, PWR-Shore power breaker, RO- Water maker, SC-Sea water chest, S-Sea water strainer, WT-Watertight doors.

SECURING EQUIPMENT
IN THE ENGINEROOM

All of the fuel piping valves are grouped together in a "manifold," usually on the forward bulkhead. They are clearly labeled and secured to the bulkhead with straps of the same material as the piping. The generator is bolted to the engine girders with steel angles as it usually has a flat mounting bed. A half-inch glass fiber box is molded to fit the number of installed batteries and it is bolted to the engine girders. Individual plastic battery boxes with tops may be purchased or a glass fiber top for the entire box may be molded. The batteries definitely have to be covered as a tool dropped on the battery may short it out, and careless yard workers may step on the batteries and cables. The bank of batteries and rectifier battery charger) should be located close to the engine starting motor so the battery cables will be as short as possible.

The sea chest shown in Figure 13 is located forward of the starboard engine. This one hull opening provides sea water for cooling the engine, transmission oil, generator, air conditioning and supply water to the reverse osmosis watermaker. All sea water piping comes from one vertical pipe of the sea chest and must be supported every thirty inches throughout its length with brackets glassed to the hull framing. The sea chest itself has four glass fiber brackets for support. As an alternative, a sea chest may be built with a copper or bronze pipe threaded to a large diameter sea cock and through hull fitting. Sea water strainers are necessary at each piece of equipment as grass can enter the system and cause a stoppage at bends in the piping.

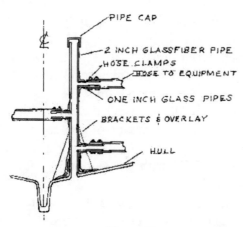

Figure 13

Detail of a fiberglass Sea Chest to permit the use of only one through hull opening. Alternately several conventional fittings and piping may be used.

75

If at all possible, watertight doors should be installed in the solid fore-and-aft bulkheads in the engineroom. If there is a break in the water piping in any part of the engineroom, the water should be confined in that area so the remainder of the boat is not affected. A large capacity bilge pump in three of four areas of the hull is also a necessity. The remainder of the equipment aft of the engines is bolted to glass fiber brackets glassed to the girders and hull framing. Use a glass laminate of three pair mat and woven roving.

EXHAUST SYSTEMS

The dry exhaust pipes the gasses directly from the engine exhaust manifold to the outside through a smoke stack on top of the boat. The stack is usually much larger than the exhaust piping and the extra volume is used to duct fresh air to the engineroom. The size of this air intake, in square inches, must be a minimum of one-third of the total installed horsepower. For example, if there is 300 horsepower, the air intake opening must be a minimum of 100 square inches. This method of calculating minimum air supply openings applies to all boats. Air is required for proper fuel combustion and for cooling the engineroom below the usual 150 degrees. The temperature of the exhaust gas may reach 850 degrees at the engine. All piping and supports must be insulated from the boat's structure. A muffler is installed either in the engineroom or inside the stack. It is a matter of preference whether you have a dry or wet exhaust system. Usually it is a matter of having the exhaust fit in with the exterior styling or having it concealed in the hull.

The wet exhaust system pipes the engine cooling water into the exhaust gas after it leaves the manifold. The piping then continues aft to the transom where the bottom of the pipe should be about six inches above the actual waterline. If possible, the highest point in the system should be at the engine exhaust manifold; if not, the exhaust piping must be run 24-inches above the actual waterline or a water lift muffler can be used. Always emphasize the entire piping system must be gas tight to avoid death to the crew.

The exhaust gas is cooled by the hot engine water, but the exhaust piping must be resistant to high temperatures and to sulfuric acid. The acid is formed when the water mixes with the sulfur in the exhaust gas. The water piping from the engine heat exchanger must be at least six inches above the actual waterline at its highest point and have a siphon break opening at the top, before entering the exhaust line.

If a water lift muffler is used, there should be at least 24 inches of vertical drop from the exhaust manifold to the muffler. If this is not possible, the dry exhaust piping between these two points will have to be run at least six inches above the actual waterline and insulated to prevent burns to the crew. The water piping from the heat exchanger then enters the exhaust line just before meeting the muffler.

When the wet exhaust does not use a water lift muffler, a purchased muffler is installed just ahead of the transom. Make sure the diameter of all components in the exhaust system is the same as the diameter at the engine exhaust manifold. It is also good practice to have a vertical surge pipe just forward of the transom and 24 inches above the exhaust outlet to prevent water from entering the line when a large following sea hits the transom.

THE PROPELLER SHAFT & RUDDER

Figure 14 shows the rudder and shaft in a customary installation and Figure 15 is a photo of the rudder installation in a sailboat. It is very important to have the rudder strongly supported on a glass or aluminum platform and have the stuffing box strongly glassed or bolted to the hull. The rudder should be as deep as the propeller in a powerboat and twice that depth in a sailboat. Powerboat rudders are usually purchased, and are made of cast bronze. Sailboat rudders can be made of glass fiber laminated around the steel rudder post and a stainless steel centerline plate. when laminating any flat section, such as a rudder, laminate slowly with the part clamped in a large vise or weighted, as the heat given off when curing will warp the flat blade. Any slight warping or bending in a rudder will be very noticeable when steering.

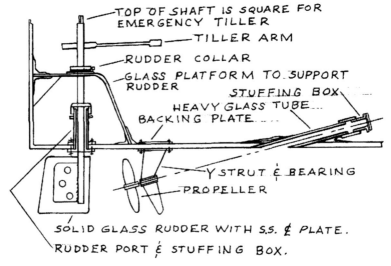

TOP OF SHAFT IS SQUARE FOR EMERGENCY TILLER
TILLER ARM
RUDDER COLLAR
GLASS PLATFORM TO SUPPORT RUDDER
STUFFING BOX
HEAVY GLASS TUBE
BACKING PLATE
Y STRUT & BEARING
PROPELLER
SOLID GLASS RUDDER WITH S.S. ℄ PLATE.
RUDDER PORT & STUFFING BOX.

Figure 14

Construction detail of the shaft tube, stuffing box, rudder port and rudder foundation.

Older boats used wire cables running over bronze sheaves to connect the steering wheel to the rudder, but these were only practical when the helm was close to the rudder. Long cable runs resulted in slack cables coming off the sheaves or misalignment of the sheaves. New boats use a patented push and pull cable in a conduit or one of the many hydraulic systems on the market. If the helm is directly over the rudder the old system of a geared quadrant is very reliable. Make sure the steering wheel is marked when the rudder is amidships. Whatever steering system you choose, make sure the steering is very solid and is checked frequently. It is very embarrassing to lose steering control as the only recourse is to steer with the engines or reverse and anchor if it is a single engine hull. Outboard motors eliminate many of these problems

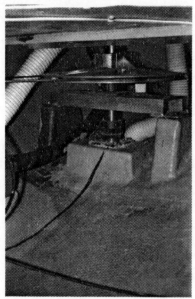

Figure 15

Rudder post detail showing the steering cable and a steel channel to support the weight of the rudder, rudder post and steering quadrant.

Extra laminate should be used in the area of the shaft struts, on the inside of the hull and about thirty inches square. Two pair of mat and woven roving is recommended. If the strut becomes loose, that engine will have to be shut down. An aluminum backing plate, one-quarter inch thick and twice the area of the rectangle formed by the four bolts is used on the inside to distribute the load. The struts must be in an area of solid glass laminate. Core material must not be used in this area. Lock washers are used under the nuts on the inside and the exposed threads will be staked so there is no possibility of loosening. A Y-strut is highly recommended as it has two struts instead of one for good rigidity and the lower piece usually protects the propeller from debris. The rubber shaft bearing inside the strut should have a plastic shell.

After the shaft strut is secured so that the calculated propeller diameter will have sufficient tip clearance, the inside shaft stuffing box is installed. A half-inch wall glass fiber tube is glassed to the hull with five pair of mat and woven roving laminate. The tube is aligned by inserting a wood shaft or the actual steel shaft, into the strut and aligning the glass fiber tube around the shaft. The stuffing box itself is secured later.

After the propeller shaft strut and the shaft tube have been installed, the engines can be aligned with the propeller shaft in place. The point of alignment is the coupling flanges on the engine transmission output shaft and on the forward end of the propeller shaft. These two flanges are brought together so they are exactly parallel, as measured with feeler gauges around the perimeter of the flanges. The feeler gauges are thin pieces of steel, machined to an exact thickness.

The engine is tilted and shifted with small hydraulic jacks until the flanges are centered and parallel with gauges of . 002 or .004 inches. Steel wedges and shim stock are used under the engine mounts to get the engine in exact alignment with the propeller shaft. At times, the steel brackets under the engine mounts must be reshaped in order to fit properly and securely.

PROPELLERS

The propeller is designed to transmit the torque of the engine into thrust in order to move the boat. In order to reduce the loading on the propeller blades and to have them operate efficiently, they must be of sufficient diameter. Longer and heavier boats require a larger diameter than shorter and lighter boats. The following table shows an approximate minimum diameter propeller required for average boats. These values will not apply to racing hulls or to boats that are very heavy.

25 ft. length - 15 inches	45 ft. length - 22 inches
30 ft. length - 16 inches	50 ft. length - 25 inches

35 ft. length - 18 inches   55 ft. length - 28 inches
40 ft. length - 20 inches   60 ft. length - 30 inches

Propeller diameter is extremely important and it is best to consult the propeller manufacturer for each installation. The retail propeller sales and repair shops can be very helpful in obtaining this information. A sailboat normally uses a two-bladed propeller for minimum resistance, but may change to a three-bladed propeller for long distance power cruising. A powerboat normally uses a three-bladed propeller but a heavier hull and boats over 45 feet in length usually have a four-bladed propeller.

The following chart shows the propeller diameter for some engine's horsepower and shaft RPM. This is simply a preliminary guide.

HORSEPOWER	PROPELLER RPM			
	600	900	1,500	2,100
	DIAMETER inches			
30	26	20	15	12
60	30	24	18	14
90	33	26	19	16
120	35	27	20	17
200	38	30	22	18
300	42	33	24	20
400	44	35	26	21

The pitch of the propeller on an average hull can be calculated from this formula: Pitch = Speed multiplied by 1800 and divided by the propeller RPM (Speed is in knots). A slow speed, displacement hull will have 20 percent more pitch and a planing hull will have 20 percent less pitch. It is normal for a ratio of propeller pitch to diameter to be 0.5 for a slow, displacement speed hull. This ratio for moderate speed hulls can be from 0.6 to 0.8, and 0.9 to 1.2 for planing hulls.

The propeller size is determined early in the design phase so clearances, engine placement and rudder location can be determined. Most important is the clearance from the top of the propeller to the hull, called "tip clearance." This should be at least 20 percent of the propeller diameter. Many boats have been a disappointment when too little tip clearance produces a thumping noise throughout the hull.

The reduction gear is in the same housing as the reverse gear and serves to reduce the RPM of the engine so that the propeller shaft is much slower turning and the correct propeller diameter can be used. A lower propeller RPM requires a larger diameter propeller with the same engine horsepower if the maximum engine RPM is not to be exceeded at wide open throttle. The reduction gear is selected at the beginning of the design calculations. For boats under forty feet in length; Planing Hull normally use a 1.5:1 gear; Average Hulls use a 2:1 gear; and Sailboats or slow Power Boats use a 2.5:1 gear.

The diameter of the propeller shaft varies with the torsional strength of the shaft material, engine horsepower and shaft RPM. The manufacturer of the shaft should be consulted for each hull, as only they know what material strength is used. The following table is an approximation of the shaft diameter required for various engine horsepower ratings and shaft RPM. The torsional strength of the material is assumed at 20,000 pounds per square inch.

HORSEPOWER	PROPELLER RPM			
	600	900	1,500	2,100
	SHAFT DIAMETER IN INCHES			
30	1.5	1.25	1.1	1
60	1.8	1.6	1.37	1.25
90	2.12	1.84	1.5	1.37
120	2.37	2	1.75	1.5
200	2.74	2.5	2	1.75
300	3.12	2.75	2.37	2
400	3.5	3	2.5	2.25

There should be some further comment on the installation of the drive train system. It is *always* convenient to remove the propeller shaft if the rudder does not have to be removed to provide shaft clearance. Keep in mind the rubber bearing in the shaft strut must be replaced about every year, depending on how many hours the boat is used. On a single engine installation, the forward part of the rudder will have to be shaped to allow the propeller shaft to pass aft without hitting the rudder blade. This curve in the leading edge of the rudder does not have any effect on the steering qualities. A hole in the rudder may also be used.

With a twin engine hull, The rudder post is set one shaft diameter either inboard or outboard of the propeller shaft so the shaft may be removed without difficulty. A keel that is deeper than the lower tip of the propeller is always recommended for both single and twin engine installations. Two keels are better than one in twin engine boats. When the unprotected propeller hits a rock, it may shear a propeller blade or even cause a hole in the boat's hull. A keel will pay for itself in one grounding.

PIPING AND WIRING IN THE ENGINEROOM

All water piping passing through the hull must have valves or sea cocks, unless you install a sea chest. There should be a soft wood plug at each sea cock in event of a break or leak. Each engine will have two fuel strainers and one sea water strainer. If a reducing fitting is required between the sea cock diameter and the heat exchanger diameter, it must be installed in a straight section of piping and never at an elbow. Copper piping is best, but if flexible hose is used, there must be two clamps at each end. Fuel piping must have a wall thickness of at least .060 inches of copper or seamless steel. Fuel shut off valves must be of an approved type and a short length only of flexible fuel line should be used at each engine to reduce the effects of vibration.

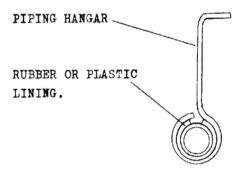

PIPING HANGAR

RUBBER OR PLASTIC
LINING.

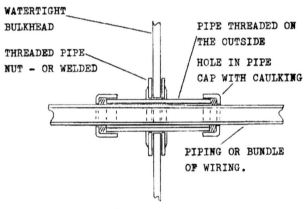

WATERTIGHT
BULKHEAD

THREADED PIPE
NUT - OR WELDED

PIPE THREADED ON
THE OUTSIDE

HOLE IN PIPE
CAP WITH CAULKING

PIPING OR BUNDLE
OF WIRING.

Figure 16 & 16a

Proper methods to support and protect piping and wiring.

Electrical wiring, instrumentation wiring and controls to the engine should all be located outboard against the side of the hull and as high as possible. All wiring and controls must be supported with clips and hangars every twenty inches. The best installation is to put all wiring inside PVC pipe to prevent chafing and damage. The wiring can be inserted inside the pipe by dropping a small lead or steel weight inside the pipe which is tied to a light nylon line. The light line is tied to the wiring and pulled through, or a fish tape can be used. A length of line should be left in each run of conduit to be used when additional wires must be pulled through the conduit. Bends in the piping are accomplished with standard or electrical conduit PVC pipe fittings. These precautionary steps should be followed throughout the boat. Vibration and chafing are the causes of most wiring and piping failures. Use hangar supports between bulkheads and use rubber or plastic sleeves at the bulkheads. When passing through a watertight bulkhead, a watertight sleeve should be used as shown in Figure 16. Keep all wiring and piping above the cabin sole whenever possible.

CHAPTER TEN
BUILDING THE DECK

DECK BEAMS

The deck may be installed before or after the interior berths and galley, as it is simply a matter of preference. You first need framing on which to work and to support the deck. You can cut transverse beams port to starboard) patterned from the loft, but some think it easier to use longitudinal beams of 1 x 2 hard wood, spaced 16 inches apart. These are supported by notches in the tops of each bulkhead. These two options may be used with decks that have a deck house, trunk cabin or are mostly flush decks.

The beams, and the thin plywood glued to the top of them, may be covered with glass on the bottom side or they may be varnished and left as a decorative overhead covering. Be certain the beams leave sufficient headroom under them. Use three-sixteenth-inch thick plywood on top of the beams, which may be exterior fir if it is to be glassed or it may have a decorative veneer on the bottom.

All of the beams are faired with a long batten to make sure the deck shape is exactly as desired. Where the ends of the beams meet the hull, they are glassed with two pair of mat and woven roving. Once again, you have to consider the attachment of the deck to the hull. If there is an outward turning flange, there is no question. Alternately, you can bring the glass deck laminate over the top edge of the hull and glass to a rough sanded surface to three inches below the sheer. Mask the hull side to prevent marking with drips of resin. Another solution occurs when there is a glass bulwark molded into the hull, and the deck level (sheer) is four to twelve inches below the top of the hull side. The two glass laminates meet in a vertical position (hull to deck) and there is a wood or aluminum cap with caulking covering the top edges of both laminates. See Figure 17. In all methods of attaching the deck to the hull, two pair of mat and woven roving are laminated on the inside to stiffen the structure at the sheer.

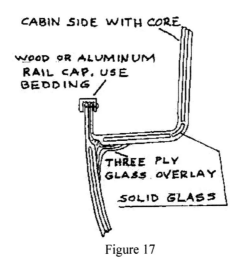

Figure 17

Joining the deck to the hull at the bulwark

Where the deck meets the bottom edge of the trunk cabin or deck house, the plywood seam may be uneven and this may be filled with polyester resin putty (resin mixed with micro balloons). Leave a one or two inch radius on the outside to prevent air entrapment in the subsequent glass laminations. Vertical wood posts, spaced sixteen inches, form the framework of the sides of the deck house and are securely bolted to the deck beams where possible. If the interior accommodations are not compromised, it is good construction to extend these vertical house side posts down to the hull where they are securely glassed. Review the construction drawings you purchased and make sure the deck and house framing is solid before covering with plywood and glass. Looking at the deck house on a cruising boat, its only support are the floor beams, bulkheads and posts below the floor. Be certain the sides and floor of the deck house are secured to the hull.

LAMINATING THE DECK

The thickness of the glass deck is specified on your drawings but is generally the same thickness as the hull bottom, outboard of the keel. This is all on top of the thin plywood if the plywood is to be exposed on the bottom. If not, the bottom of the thin plywood is covered with one mat and one layer of six-ounce cloth. The latter gives a smoother finished appearance. The remainder of the required laminate is put on the top of the thin plywood. Take care not to put your full body weight on the thin plywood before the glass has completely cured. Support your weight with heavier plywood planks temporarily placed on the beams. Take ample time with the deck laminate as any imperfections must be repaired at a later time. Where the deck meets the hull laminate, they must be rolled together so the laminate is absolutely flat. The laminate has a tendency to become separated at this joint and it may be necessary to use clamps and boards covered with wax paper to hold the glass flat until it cures.

Follow the same procedures as when laminating the hull. It may be wise to use less hardener in the resin to give you more time to roll out the deck laminate. Laminating the deck proceeds slowly as you must bring the glass up the sides of the deck house or trunk cabin and you probably will not complete the laminate in one day. Use a layer of peel ply without extra resin between periods of laminating.

The finish of the deck is tedious as it must be carefully completed. The appearance of the boat is largely judged on the finish of the deck, as this is what people see from the dock or from another boat. At the same time the flat portions of the deck must have a nonskid texture. This can be accomplished with a paint that has special sand dropped onto it while still wet. Also, there are nonskid paints available on the market which can be rolled on without much difficulty. There are also composite plastic, nonskid sheets that can be glued to the laminate in various patterns.

CHAPTER ELEVEN
BUILDING WITHOUT DRAWINGS

During this discussion of building the deck and hull -- or buying a bare glass hull -- I have assumed you have purchased a set of drawings that tell you how to proceed. This chapter will explain what to do if those drawings are not available. Actually, it is money well spent to have a boat designer prepare your drawings and to explain exactly what must be accomplished. Professional advice is always worthwhile.

When you attempt to draw your arrangement for the interior of the hull, you are certainly free to install whatever equipment you would like, but you have to make sure the boat will float level and in proper trim. In the design stages, this is accomplished by calculating the center of gravity (CG) of all items in the boat. The total CG of all items must be in the same longitudinal position as the center of buoyancy (LCB). The LCB is the center of the submerged volume of the hull and is carefully calculated by the designer. The LCB is usually noted on the hull lines you purchased and occurs normally between 53 percent and 58 percent of the waterline length from the forward end of the waterline as designed. See Figure 18. If you do not know the exact position of the hull LCB, you can use 55 percent for an average hull, 53 percent for slower boats and 58 percent of the waterline length for planing hulls. Since this position of the hull LCB is approximate, you will have to move weights or add ballast after the boat is completed in order to achieve level trim.

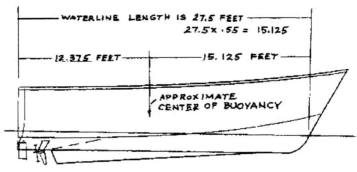

Figure 18

Estimating the position of the longitudinal center of buoyancy.

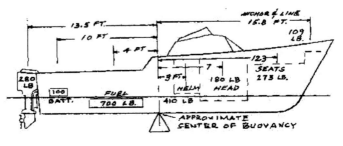

Figure 19

Examples of weight influence on the trim of the boat.

The problem in achieving level trim is one of the old seesaw as shown in Figure 19. Each weight in pounds is multiplied by its distance from the assumed LCB and the total of these multiplication's for each item, forward minus aft, is zero. For example, Figure 19 shows an open boat with outboard motor, console and a head. Multiplying the equipment weight by its distance from the assumed LCB: motor (280 x 13.5 = 3780) plus batteries (100 x 10 = 1000) plus fuel tank (700 x 4 = 2800). This totals 7580 foot-pounds aft of the assumed LCB. Doing the same multiplication's for those items forward of the LCB, we have: anchors and lines (109 x 15.8 = 1722), seats (273 x 12.3 = 3350), head (180 x 7 = 1260) and helm console (410 x 3 = 1230). These total 7570 foot-pounds forward of the LCB and the boat is in level trim since the moment of items forward equals the moment of items aft. This procedure is the same for all types and lengths of hulls.

We now move to another example of calculating trim for a boat. If the engines and mounts are 3000 pounds and 2.6 feet aft of the LCB (7800 foot-pounds), the anchor and windlass are 290 pounds and 21 feet forward of the LCB (6090 foot-pounds), and the head, fixtures and bulkheads arc 205 pounds and 8.34 feet forward of the LCB (1710 foot-pounds), the total is zero. (7800 aft = 6090 + 1710 forward). This is further explained in Figure 22, where all of the weights in a 33-foot hull are listed so the total center of gravity is shown at the LCB. Two boats are illustrated: one is a normal family cruising boat and the other is a SCUBA dive boat on the same hull. See Figures 20 and 21 which show their arrangement.

The listing of weights and distances (Figure 22) from an assumed Center of Buoyancy is just one example of how to proceed. The primary point to remember is the hull pivots or adjusts trim, at a point (LCB) that is the center of the volume of the portion of the hull below the waterline. When any large weights are added to the hull or a cargo is carried temporarily, the effect on trim must be carefully considered. A boat out of trim will steer poorly and may become unsafe in a seaway. Good calculations save a lot of manual labor.

Building a sailboat from a bare hull without proper drawings follows the same procedure except for ballast and mast location. It is prudent to install only half the ballast at first, until the boat is completed and the trim can be studied. The mast, boom and rigging weight is best located from the experience of those who have built from the same hull. It is a necessity to talk with other owners to be certain you do not make mistakes.

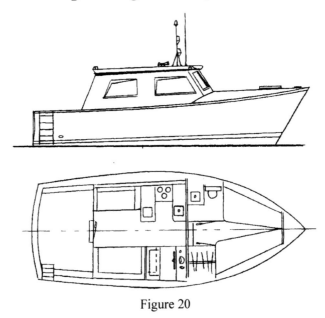

Figure 20

An average 33-foot cruising boat.

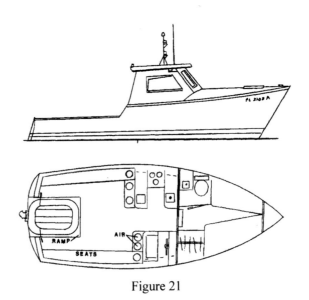

Figure 21

A 33-foot SCUBA dive boat.

CALCULATIONS FOR TRIM ON A 33-FOOT HULL				
ITEMS ON A CRUISING HULL	WEIGHT POUNDS	FT AFT OR FWD OF ASSUMED LCB	FT X WT FWD	FT X WT AFT
Hull	4,000	1.2 A		4,800
Deck	2,250	1 F	2,250	
Bulkheads	250	1.2 F	300	
Framing	880	1 F	880	
Two engines	3,050	0.2 F	610	
Batteries	220	1.4 A		308
Steering	320	0.8 A		256
Shafts & Struts	500	7.2 A		3,600
Props & Rudders	280	10.5 A		2,940
Exhausts	220	7.5 A		1,650
3 Tanks	450	6.5 A		2,925
Electrical	180	3.5 F	630	
Plumbing	150	2.5 F	375	
Anchor	50	12F	600	
Deck Hardware	200	9-5 F	1,900	
Windows	180	1.8 F	324	
Helm & Console	120	4 F	480	
Berths	380	12F	4,560	
Lockers	320	6.5 F	1,430	
Galley	250	2.2 F	550	
Head	250	7F	1,750	
Lounge Seats	120	3 A		360
Hullside Coverings	180	1.5 F	270	
Cruising Hull Totals	14,800		16,839	16,839
33-foot Dive Boat	ABOVE WEIGHTS PLUS THE FOLLOWING			
Aft Tanks	280	0.5A		140
Dinghy	250	10A		2,500
Ballast	220	12F	2,640	
Dive Boat Totals	15,550		19,479	19,479

Figure 22

Note that in Figure 22 the moments aft and forward of the LCB are equal. indicating level trim.

CHAPTER TWELVE
HATCHES, WINDOWS & VENTILATION

HATCHES

We must provide access hatches to the anchors, engines, rudders and emergency exits from all interior spaces. Nothing is more annoying than a leaking hatch and the installation must be watertight and permanent. Don't cut corners on the quality of hatches or windows. It is more expensive, but installation time is reduced if manufactured hatches are purchased. The hatches made by Bomar, Beckson, Freeman, Vetus and other fine manufacturers are good quality and made in a variety of shapes and sizes. You can make your hatches with a wood frame of teak or cypress that does not rot, as shown in Figure 23, with ample bedding compound at the seams. On the side opposite the hinge, use a nut and bolt type of latch to secure the hatch from inside the boat. Locks and screens are a necessity.

Plan the location of all hatches and windows carefully so they will not interfere with the deck beams or bulkheads below the deck. Often, deck beams must be cut and a box frame of doubled deck beams will have to be built around the hatch opening. Deck lockers are usually made with watertight, hinged tops for stowage of lines and fenders and they must be watertight to the deck and to the cabin side.

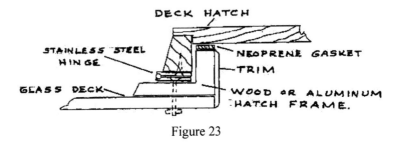

Figure 23

Proper construction of a raised deck hatch.

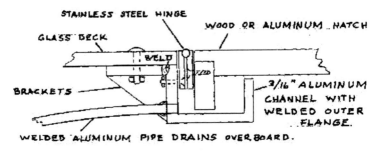

Figure 24

Proper construction of a flush deck hatch.

If you want exterior hatches that are flush to the deck, as at the rudders and over the engines, you have a complicated piece of wood or aluminum construction, unless you use a manufactured hatch. See Figure 24. The hatch must be solid enough to walk on frequently and it must have drain grooves and piping to prevent water from entering the boat. Below decks, there must be removable posts to support the wide expanse of hatch to keep it from flexing. Permanent hatch supports must hold the hatch open when desired in order to prevent injury to the crew. This support may be like the car hood support or it may be a sliding rod held by a friction clamp. If there is a hatch in a built-in seat, such as in a sailboat cockpit, it also must have drain grooves installed that slope to the deck, where the deck drains remove the water. This construction is similar to Figure 24, except the channel slopes down to drain excess water. Hatches are always difficult to make watertight and bedding compound or rubber gasket material must be used to conform to the irregularities of the deck.

WINDOWS

Manufactured windows and portlights are only made in a few shapes, but they are strong, watertight and usually offer the easiest installation. If you want elongated or curved shapes you can cut the cabin side opening to any desired form and locate the safety plate glass inboard of a watertight gasket. This is illustrated in Figure 25. Basically, the window construction is a rectangular frame of glass fiber flat panels (flat bar) that is glassed to the inside of the cabin side. A trim piece or keeper, is screwed to the glass fiber frame with caulking and holds the window in position. The safety plate glass is not cut to the shape of the window opening, but is rectangular and fits exactly to the glass fiber frame. These are fixed windows that do not open.

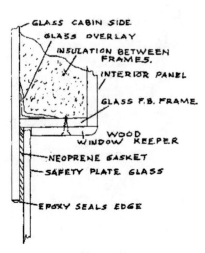

Figure 25

Proper cabin side window construction.

Opening windows are difficult for the owner to fabricate and a great amount of time is saved by purchasing from the manufacturers. They use extruded aluminum frames with matching extruded rubber gaskets and the combination produces an excellent product. There are some fine marine window manufacturers in the USA and the marine supply stores can order what you want. Sliding windows are hardly ever watertight, but offer the advantage that swinging room is not required for a hinged window. Whatever window you use, be sure to have screens and secure locks on the inside. In any port, flies and larger vermin will always try to enter the boat.

Figure 26 shows one suggestion for an owner built opening windshield window. It is basically a safety plate glass window in an aluminum frame. No attempt is made to pull the window tightly against a gasket, but water leaks are drained in an aluminum channel. Either mechanical or electric windshield wipers are mounted on the glass fiber framing above the window.

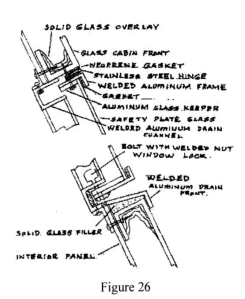

Figure 26

Opening windshield section with water drain channels.

In an enclosed helm area there must be ventilation in the form of an opening section of windshield, an installed vent cowl or an opening hatch in the roof over the steering wheel. The sun on the windshield causes a severe temperature rise and the area becomes extremely uncomfortable without good ventilation. when you have to spend many hours at the helm, you should certainly make sure it will be as comfortable as possible.

In many cases it is money well spent to have a windshield custom fit and welded exactly to fit your requirements. This is especially true when there are many glass panels and the windshield extends from one side of the deck house to the other. Boat windshield manufacturers have a specialized, custom business that is usually located near a large boat manufacturer. They can be found in the Yellow Pages or by talking with a boat repair yard. If you build a boat without a top over the helm, make provisions for a removable top as it will be very uncomfortable when it is raining, very hot or very cold. A permanent top over the helm is always recommended.

VENTILATION

It is important to have good air circulation inside the boat. On a cruise, the air can become very stale and the crew will develop headaches if there are not sufficient air intakes. In the humid Florida climate, mildew grows rapidly on most surfaces when the air is not circulated. When underway, hatches can be opened and the boat becomes pleasant. But we are most concerned with the eighty percent of the boat's life spent at the dock.

There are many water-trap type of ventilators on the market that are mounted on the deck, cabin top or on a hatch; wherever they do not interfere with the operation of the boat. They are a vital part of enjoying boating as any experienced owner will testify. Unfortunately, they are usually ignored by manufacturers and you will not see them in the glossy magazine advertisements. Probably, they don't want to add to the cost of the boat and they wrongly assume that the boat will be operated in a cool climate or have the air conditioning running.

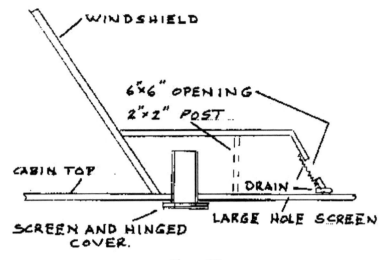

Figure 27

Vent box construction to provide air to the boat's interior, The box may span the width of the cabin top to serve several areas.

It is a necessity to have good ventilation in the head. A water-trap vent should be placed over the shower so the humid and fragrant air can be displaced. In addition, a water-trap vent box can be built on the deck or cabin top, just below the windshield, as shown in Figure 27. This is simply a box with air holes in the forward face and two or three water drains. A PVC or aluminum, six inch diameter, pipe ducts fresh air to the interior. It has a hinged cover to block air when it is too cold. This vent box can be twelve inches wide with one vent or several feet wide with three or four air ducts to different compartments.

It is poor practice to have opening portlights in the hull side, below the sheer. Someone is always leaving one open and unusual waves or wakes from other boats have a way of entering your boat when you least expect it. Air circulation must be provided from vents on deck and not from opening portlights. I know of one large motor yacht that ran aground and heeled over about seventy degrees. Water entered the open portlights and the boat sunk with one side on the bottom. A fortune was spent in re-floating and rebuilding the boat. The portlights were welded shut.

ENGINEROOM AIR

One of the problems facing engine manufacturers is most boat builders do not provide sufficient air intakes to the engines for complete combustion of the fuel. The engines are then operating at less than designed horsepower and the owner wonders why his boat is so much slower than another with the same engines.

I responded to a similar complaint by an owner. Upon entering the engineroom one morning, the temperature was about 130 degrees even though the engines had not been used for 18 hours. It was obvious there was little air circulation in the engineroom either for fuel combustion or for cooling the surrounding spaces.

The air supply to the engineroom should come from the outside of the deck house (cabin side) above the sheer. Air intakes in the hull side below the sheer are poor practice. There have been many cases of low freeboard sportfisherman trolling in the trough of waves and rolling to the point where water enters the hull side air vent. The minimum air vent opening in square inches, on each side, is one-third the total horsepower. For example, if there are two, 300 horsepower engines, the minimum air vent opening is 200 square inches. A 10 inch by 20 inch opening is not excessive in appearance. A wood box duct takes the air below to the engineroom. This can be concealed outboard under a seat.

Natural air circulation is good, but a continuous duty intake fan is better. The capacity of this fan should be three times the total horsepower, in cubic feet per minute. With large engines it is good to have a small exhaust fan in the engineroom aft bulkhead which is used for an hour or two to remove engine heat after the engines have been secured for the day. If the engineroom is amidships, a fan and duct to the main deck can be used, but do not use the intake air duct for the exhaust fan. When a sailboat engine is located under the cockpit, low profile, water-trap cowl ventilators can be used on the side or lazarette decks. These vents can be as small as three inches high and are available from various manufacturers.

CHAPTER THIRTEEN
DECK HARDWARE

ANCHORS

Starting at the bow, we have to take a long look at the anchor and rode, a subject often overlooked by the manufacturers. Possibly, this is because most owners use their boat for a few hours on a weekend afternoon and never use the anchor. Good seamanship dictates that anchoring is a necessity for your own protection, as well as a convenience when cruising. If the engine fails, you must use the anchor to hold the boat away from the rocks while you attempt repairs. If you have left the dock lines on the dock and are in need of a tow or need to tow another boat, you will need the anchor rode.

If your boat is under forty feet in length, it is usually easy to lift a twenty-two-pound anchor onto the deck and tie it to anchor chocks. This is a normal arrangement, but it is inconvenient to stumble over the anchor when putting out dock lines or to have the dock lines get tangled in the flukes. It is much neater to install a flush deck hatch at the bow, with a watertight, glass fiber box, glassed to the underside of the deck. Two anchors and rodes can be stowed in this anchor locker. The locker can be twelve to eighteen inches deep and extend forty to fifty inches aft of the stem, at the deck.

Below this anchor locker, there is a small, prism shaped volume that is normally stuffed with excess gear, with access from the forward V-berths. It is much better to use this compartment as an important, water tight, foam-filled safety structure. This extends to the bottom of the hull with a watertight, vertical bulkhead at the aft end of the anchor locker and foam-filled compartment. If a boat is in a collision or hits a rock or log, it is usually at the waterline at the stem. This foam compartment may help confine the damage to one area and prevent water migration to the rest of the hull; a great safety feature.

Anchor and dock lines should be at least three-eighths of an inch diameter Nylon on boats to thirty feet and half-inch diameter Nylon on boats between thirty and forty feet in length. Dock lines and fenders must be stowed on deck in their own locker, usually aft, under the cockpit rail or under the seats. If you like SCUBA, fishing or water skiing, it is wise to plan ahead and provide secure lockers for all the gear. When the boat is in rough water or wakes, you don't want anything sliding across the deck. Be certain to have clearly marked life jacket stowage on deck for each member of the crew. This is a legal requirement.

An anchor windlass is very convenient on larger hulls and when body strength is not available. They may be manual or 12 VDC electric. Often, the anchor may become snagged on the bottom and you may not have enough sea room to run the boat up over the anchor and drag it loose with the engines. This is when the windlass pays for itself. I was on a sixty-foot motor yacht which had to be brought alongside a dock with a thirty-knot wind blowing directly off the dock. No amount of maneuvering with the engines brought the boat within spitting distance. It was after midnight and no one was on the dock to provide assistance. I finally managed to throw a loop of line over a dock cleat and put one end on a deck cleat and the other end on the electric windlass. Pulling on this line and later on a breast line finally brought the boat to the pier. The windlass motor was hot after a half-hour's use, but it really saved us from an embarrassing situation.

The windlass should have a 200-pound pull on boats under thirty feet and a 500-pound pull on boats between thirty and forty feet, as a minimum. Manual anchor windlasses must have a mechanical advantage ratio of at least 20:1. This means that if you push on the end of the handle with thirty pounds, there will be a 600-pound force pulling on the line. There are many fine manufacturers of both types of winches. The stainless steel manual winches are good quality.

Many boats have a bow roller at the stem on deck to keep the line from chafing the hull while lowering or raising the anchor and to keep it on the boat's centerline. The last few feet of raising the anchor will bring the flukes close to the hull with the chance of scratching the hull finish. This can usually be prevented by installing a U-shaped bracket that extends about eighteen inches forward of the stem, about eighteen inches wide with side supports to the hull. This can be fabricate from schedule 80 stainless steel pipe or solid glass fiber rod. This bracket is bolted or heavily glassed to the hull after custom fitting to the hull shape. The anchor bracket catches the anchor flukes as it is raised and can be used to permanently store the anchor when it is not in use and when the anchor is too heavy to lift off of the bow roller. Many manufactured boats have an anchor platform at the stem. Used with a bow roller, this is a very good method of keeping the anchor away from the hull. Stainless steel pipe in a "U" shape is normally used for the platform that extends twenty-four to thirty-six inches forward of the stem.

GETTING ABOARD THE BOAT

Climbing over the high topsides of most boats is very difficult and there must be a ladder or platform to use after swimming or, more importantly, when someone falls overboard. Even a twenty-foot hull has enough freeboard to make boarding difficult. A portable ladder tied to the deck cleats is only partially convenient as the lower step moves under the bottom of the hull when it is used, making it difficult to raise a leg to the other steps. Some assistance from the crew is required.

Probably the best solution is to install a stern platform on the transom just above the exhaust outlets. This can be teak supported by bronze angle brackets or it can be a stainless steel pipe platform and brackets with a teak grating on top. Since it is just a few inches above the water, it is much easier to roll onto rather than climb a ladder. The swim platform is eighteen to thirty inches wide and can be used on a sport fisherman for boarding a fish instead of reaching over the stern rail. The platform is a valuable addition to any boat.

A sailboat usually has a narrow transom with the bottom edge well above the waterline, thus making a swim platform impractical. Whether the transom slopes forward or aft, there are some clever stainless steel ladders on the market. These are double hinged, with brackets, so there is a lower section extending below the waterline about two feet and an upper section that reaches from the bottom of the transom to the deck level. Of course, if boat davits are installed at the stern and the dinghy is put into the water, it can be used for a good exit from the water. Often, a stainless steel ladder can be installed at the transom next to outboard motors, with brackets to the hull to support a lower step. Make sure the motors are not running when swimmers are attempting to board the boat. It is easy for a foot to slip.

CLEATS, CHOCKS & OTHER FITTINGS

It is not good practice to reduce costs by using small diameter lines and it is worse to use small cleats and chocks. Nine-inch cleats on a boat under thirty feet are suitable and twelve-inch cleats should be used on hulls between thirty and forty feet. Smaller cleats do not have enough space underneath to wrap the lines two or three times around. Beware of Nylon lines on the smooth finish of a cleat when the line gets old and hard. The line will slip fight off the cleat if there is not a half hitch around one end of the cleat. Sometimes there is no friction at all!

All hardware should have four mounting holes with four through bolts. Screws will just not hold. At the dock, chocks get pulled sideways when wakes bounce the boat and put heavy strain on the dock lines. Lifeline stanchions get pushed out of line when a person leans on them. You can not be too careful with through bolted hardware.

Chocks keep the dock lines from rubbing on the hull and guide the lines to the cleats. They should be located out board of each cleat, with at least two forward, two amidships and two at the stern. You may often need a midships breast line and the cleat is always handy to attach fenders. You may want to install additional cleats and chocks to accommodate fenders where they are most often used. On sportfisherman, it is inconvenient to have cleats on the stern rail as they will snag fishing lines and gear. These boats usually have inboard cleats bolted to the hull and with closed chocks (scuppers) guiding the line and to prevent chafe on the rail. These scuppers (chocks) are located at cockpit deck level and are readily available at marine supply stores. They are made in two halves (one inboard and one outboard) bolted together with machine screws. Don't forget to seal the hullside laminate with resin to prevent water migration.

Some owners like the forward cleats near the boat centerline so the cleats can be used for the anchor line as well. Others like the cleats outboard near the chocks so the deck is clear of any obstruction. Whatever you decide, arrange the bow hardware, anchor, hatches and windlass carefully so that you will have an efficient foredeck. It has to be done correctly the first time.

Many boats locate the fuel and water fill pipes outboard near the sheer. There are usually separate fill and vent pipes for each tank, located on both sides of the hull. We want to prevent accidental mistakes of water and debris entering these pipes and wherever they are located, they should be raised at least one inch above deck level. Vents may be installed on the cabin side (house side) with a clam shell type of fitting and screen to avoid contamination.

There is a great tendency to avoid the lazarette where excess gear, lines, steering and the exhausts are located. If the engines are just forward of the transom or if there are outboard motors, there is no lazarette. The rudder post stuffing box (water seal) should be checked weekly to see there is no water entering the boat. Since the rudder post is a good potential source of leaks, there should be a watertight bulkhead between the lazarette and the rest of the boat, just as at the bow. The rudder may be hit by a log or other debris, which may bend the rudder post and a leak will develop. Always check the exhaust and muffler lines to be certain all sections and fittings are airtight.

NAVIGATION AIDS

The navigation lights a boat is required to carry are described in a book called Navigation Rules (COMDINST M 16672.2C) published by the U.S. Coast Guard, available from the Superintendent of Documents, P.O. Box 371954, Pittsburgh PA 15250-7954. Phone 202-783-3238. Be sure to purchase a copy. Lights for all ships and boats are described in this publication, but I will just briefly mention the lights for vessels under twelve meters (39 feet), which are requirements at the time of this book's printing.

Basically, a boat under thirty-nine feet must have two sidelights, red to port and green to starboard, visible for a distance of one mile. They only show a light 112.5 degrees (ten points) forward, on one side of the boat centerline. They must be above the deck (sheer) but not higher than three-quarters the height of the masthead light above the deck (sheer). The masthead light must be visible for a distance of two miles and show only in the forward 225 degrees (twenty points) of the hull. This masthead light must be at least 40 inches (one meter) above the sheer (deck) and, if practical, located in the forward half of the boat. In addition, a fourth light must be located at the stern, visible for a distance of two miles aft and showing over an unbroken arc of 135 degrees (twelve points). Please consult the newest instruction book for alternative required lights for fishing boats, boats anchored, sailboats and for boats engaged in diving operations.

Radar is an expensive addition to any boat, but it is one

of the best safety devices will prove to be a lifesaver when cruising in fog, rain or at night. The waterways are more crowded every year and we must be on the lookout for ships, commercial vessels and high-speed boats with inexperienced operators. The radar antenna is located as high as possible on the boat to reduce the sea return blank area. Whether on deck or on the cabin top, it is usually necessary to locate this antenna on a platform (radar arch) in order to avoid blockage from the horn, searchlight, light mast and other hardware. This platform can be built from a glass fiber, flat panel molding, about one-quarter to three-eighths inches thick or from stainless steel pipe (schedule 40). The platform must be custom made to fit the deck or cabin top. Both the navigation lights and radar should be activated by separate batteries from the engine starting battery, as both the lights and radar are on continuously at night. All of these electrical loads are vital to the operation of the boat and you cannot afford to have them fail due to a dead battery.

Building A Fiberglass Boat by Arthur Edmunds

CHAPTER FOURTEEN
ELECTRICAL SYSTEMS

DIRECT CURRENT (DC)

Electrical power from batteries is direct current (DC) and it supplies the engine starting motor, navigation lights, electronics, bilge pumps, horn, interior lights, compass light, autopilot, windshield wipers and sometimes an inverter to produce limited alternating current (AC) power. The batteries are charged by the alternator on the engine or by a battery charger (rectifier) when using AC power from the dock In fact, the DC system is very similar to that on an automobile. The boat batteries must be checked with a hygrometer weekly, to make sure the specific gravity of the acid in the cells is sufficient or if charging is required. Only distilled water should be added to bring the electrolyte to the proper level.

The batteries are wired (connected) in parallel so each positive terminal is connected to other positive terminals and negative to negative terminals. In this manner, 12 volts DC will be produced from 12 volt batteries, but the available current (amperes) will be greatly increased. A complete description of battery use, DC and AC circuits and installation can be found in the excellent book, *Boat Repair Made Easy - Systems* by John P. Kaufman, 1996, Bristol Fashion Publications, Enola, PA 17025-0020. Phone 800-478-7147. This is a worthwhile book for all electrical system projects.

Essentially, the engine alternator is wired to the battery selector switch and an isolator (battery combiner) provides an electronic circuit that allows one set of batteries to be charged even if another set of batteries is fully charged. It is best to keep one battery solely for starting the engine and also have two other sets of batteries designated for the various circuits throughout the boat. If an inverter is used for short periods for alternating current (AC) power, one set of many batteries is usually provided for this load. You should check frequently to see if unnecessary circuits are off when not running the engine. When sailing at night, the owner often forgets to turn off the four navigation lights, panel light and compass light at sunrise. This is seven amperes used hourly.

APPROXIMATE AMPERES REQUIRED (CURRENT)	
ITEM	DRAW
Panel Lights	2 A
Radiotelephone (VHF)	2 - 6 A
Compass Light	1 A
Electronics	3 - 5 A
Deck/Cabin lights	2 A
Autopilot	3 - 5 A
Searchlight	5 - 20 A
Bilge Pump (ea.)	4 - 10 A
Windlass	40 - 120 A
Electric Toilet	20 - 30 A
Side & Mast Lights	1.3 A ea.
Watermaker	4 - 10 A
Wipers	7 A
Horn	4 - 5 A
Radar	4 - 15 A
Stereo	2 - 6 A

Figure 28

Equipment requirements vary with each supplier.

Don't cut short the number of circuit breakers on the DC electrical distribution panel. Each circuit breaker protects and isolates the lamp or equipment on that circuit, so that repair is made easier in event of a water leak and short circuit. All equipment drawing four amperes or more should be on a separate circuit breaker. Figure 28, lists the approximate ampere loads of some items.

Each circuit breaker rating should be about three to five amperes above the equipment it protects. Circuits can be combined for interior lights such as Cabin Lights Forward and Cabin Lights Aft. There are many good distribution panels on the market and they save time and add a professional touch. Add the current rating (amperes) of all DC equipment in the boat to determine the rating of the main circuit breaker in the distribution panel. All connections in the boat should have crimped terminals with heat shrink tubing. Wire nuts must not be used as they will loosen with vibration. Keep all wiring above the cabin sole and preferably at the height of the sheer, hidden behind shelves or joinerwork, yet accessible for any repairs. When wiring passes through joinerwork or bulkheads, a plastic sleeve protects the wiring from rubbing against the rough edges of the wood. Watertight wiring sleeves can be purchased for use in watertight bulkheads.

ALTERNATING CURRENT (AC)

The alternating current (AC) in your boat is identical to that in your house and the same wiring requirements and safety precautions should be followed. On a boat you will have switch gear to select the AC power source from the dock power, an onboard AC generator or an inverter. You must have a circuit breaker on the boat located between the switch gear and the dock power plug equal to the ampere rating of the main circuit breaker on the boat. This protects the boat in the event of a short circuit at the dock power connections.

All of the AC loads should be added to determine the amperage rating of the main circuit breaker. The following are the approximate current (amperes) requirements of some common appliances:

APPROXIMATE AMPERES REQUIRED (CURRENT)	
ITEM	DRAW
Oven	20 - 30 A
Range	3 - 7 A ea. burner
Refrigerator	4 - 10 A
Microwave	8 - 12 A
Dishwasher	4 A
Television	4 A
Clothes Washer	9 A
Clothes Dryer	25 A
Hot Water Heater	15 - 40 A
6 Lamps	9A
A/C Compressor	15 - 25 A
Stereo	3 - 5 A
Toaster	9 A
A/C Fan Motor	5 A

Figure 28 a

Equipment requirements vary with each supplier.

Often, only a few AC circuits are in use, but the amperage of the main circuit breaker should be selected for the maximum, with every circuit turned on. This was forcibly brought home to me when our electric utility company installed a monitoring meter and transponder at my house. During the additional wiring, the main circuit breaker was found to be charred and the plastic housing was cracked and falling apart. The building inspector said it was due to frequent overloads. I then added all the amperes of every appliance in the house and found it to be well above the circuit breaker rating of 200 amperes. This situation can occur when dinner is prepared using the oven and range while the laundry is being washed and dried with the air conditioning running and the hot water heater in use, all at the same time. Many houses burn because of an electrical overload and boats can do the same.

Please note the largest consumers of electricity are the resistance heating appliances. These are; toasters, curling irons, hair dryers, ranges, ovens of all types, electric heaters, clothes dryers and hot water heaters. Most people find it comfortable to do without these comforts of home while on a small boat for a few days cruising. If you have a large boat and plan to have an all electric home with all the above listed appliances, be sure to plan carefully, choose the generator with care, keeping in mind how many hours the generator will be used every day. Many people plan their cruising so they will be at a dock with electric power every night.

CHAPTER FIFTEEN
INTERIOR JOINERWORK

INTERIOR ARRANGEMENT

All larger boats, have some form of a galley, head and berth. The galley may include an oven and refrigerator but may also be a simple one-burner, alcohol fueled cooker and an icebox. Berths have to be at least 26 inches wide at the head and 21 inches wide at the foot. These are just minimums and 32 inches wide is much more comfortable. As seen in Figure 29, the berth can be wider if it is higher above the cabin sole, as the hull is wider at the sheer (deck). But we must allow 26 to 30 inches of space above the berth to sit upright. A berth height of 28 to 32 inches above the sole is not too high to climb into.

If you plan upper and lower berths, there must be at least 81 inches of headroom above the cabin sole. The lower berth is 19 inches above the sole. There must be about 26 inches above each berth. The upper berth is about ten inches thick, including mattress and framing. The mattress is normally urethane foam, five to six inches thick. Shaped and fitted sheets are available from many suppliers, patterned for each berth or you can make your own from standard sheets.

Storage space is always desirable and lockers under each berth are a must. Shelves over each berth are always full and a stack of drawers fifteen inches wide are a welcome addition, as well as drawers in the head. when possible, each person should have a twelve inch width of closet space and there should be a separate locker for foul weather gear. Crew items are not stowed under the cabin sole as this area is normally reserved for tanks, canned food or foam flotation in small outboard areas. Water penetration into the storage areas should not be a problem as the bilges of a glass fiber hull should be dry at all times. If not, look for the leak and repair it, usually occurring at the windows or at the deck to hull joint. In any case, a bilge pump is necessary between adjoining bulkheads in case of accident.

Each owner will have different thoughts about arrangements, but if you purchase a set of drawings, look carefully and try to realize why the designer made the arrangement in a specific manner. Remember, the balance and trim of the boat are of vital importance and you can't change the arrangement without these calculations. Minor changes can be accomplished such as having twin or double beds at the bow and these may be aft of a head if they are twin beds. In small boats, it is sometimes convenient to use a four-berth arrangement amidships, as seen on narrow beam sailboats for many years. This has a berth and a shelf outboard about thirty-six inches above the cabin sole. Just inboard of this is a combination sette/berth where the exposed mattress is about eighteen inches wide and slides inboard to make a berth width of 28 inches. The inboard sliding berth is about eighteen inches above the cabin sole. Many times, if the beam permits, there is a drop leaf table permanently mounted on the boat centerline and often on top of the centerboard trunk or around the mast.

Aft, the arrangement is planned around the engine location, which can be at the stem or almost amidships. In a small boat you may have outboard motors bolted to the transom or you may have inboard engines just forward of the transom turning outdrives (Z drives) or V drives. This clears the aft deck and allows good access to the engines and batteries. The main point is to have the engine area watertight to the rest of the boat. If there is a water leak, you don't want flooding to all parts of the hull. When the inboard engines are located well forward of the transom, engine boxes may cover each installation, with a walkway on centerline. This makes a convenient arrangement in a semi-enclosed boat, leaving a clear deck aft of the engines.

When the hull is larger than forty feet, some owners may want a private stateroom and head aft, with the engineroom located amidships. This has been popular in trawler yacht and other models. It works very well as long as there are watertight bulkheads with sound deadening insulation. The sound insulation may be purchased from specialists and usually consists of a sixteenth-inch lead sheet bonded to plastic foam that is heat resistant and which has a heat reflective surface on the other side. This sheet lead is not toxic as it is not in small particles; it is used worldwide in x-ray labs and radioactive facilities.

BUILD A MODEL INTERIOR

If you are undecided about how the interior arrangement is going to fit in the hull, why not make a trial run with disposable materials?

Obtain large, corrugated cardboard boxes in which furniture or appliances had been packed for shipping. Carefully measure all the joinerwork, cabinetry and appliances you would like to install. Reproduce these dimensions with the corrugated cardboard boxes and actually install these boxes to show all of the interior. This is done with tape, glue, staples and temporary wood bracing to hold the cardboard in place.

You will see all the problems, where the cabinets will be glassed to the hull, where the plumbing will be located and where shelves and cabinets can actually be placed. Walk around this mock interior to see how it fits, especially in close areas such as in the head. The swing of doors and sliding of drawers can be checked for any interference. It may be well to leave the cardboard in place and think about it daily, to see if any new ideas develop. when you are satisfied this is exactly what you want and no improvements can be made, proceed to cut the joiner materials and make the installation permanent. This procedure will insure major mistakes will be avoided and you will have confidence in the best arrangement possible.

ATTACHMENT TO THE GLASS HULL

It is important to overlay all joinerwork to the hull on both sides with two mat and two woven roving, as seen in Figures 29 and 30. In this manner, the shelves and countertops act as framing members to stiffen the hull and additional framing may not be required on the hull sides. The engine girder extensions forward are overlaid to the hull and support the hull as well as the cabin sole above them. Attachment of decorative interior paneling may be accomplished by overlaying wood blocks to the hull to hold screws for the trim installation. Piping hangars and equipment in the engineroom are best secured with bolts to a heavy glass angle overlaid to the hull.

BUILDING WITH "GREEN" MATERIALS

The traditional boat interior is made with wood, but there are other options. In Europe, some boats are built "green" with all recyclable, man-made materials. Diminishing natural resources are avoided, if possible. We will discuss the options of using aluminum, solid glass fiber and plastic core materials. All of these are usually more expensive than a plywood interior, depending on the surface finish.

SOLID GLASS

Flat panels of solid glass fiber are easily laminated to any thickness and they are joined by glass overlay to the cabinetry and hull. Solid glass bulkheads should be one-quarter inch in thickness and stiffened by 2 x 2 x 1/8 glass angles spaced twenty inches apart. Any decorative covering can be applied to the glass surfaces. Plastic doors and drawers are readily available. The tops of galley counters can be surfaced with sheet stainless steel, if desired, and stainless steel sinks are always recommended. Cabin soles can be sheets of glass fiber overlaid to the hull and supported by solid glass stiffeners underneath, usually by the extension of the engine girders. Carpeting is normally used over glass cabin soles. One may not think of glass fiber being a recyclable material, but it can be ground into small pieces for use as a reinforcement in road surfaces. Since most glass fiber hulls and decks have a life span of over fifty years, they do not present a problem.

ALUMINUM INTERIORS

It may be unthinkable for some traditionalists to attempt an aluminum interior in a glass fiber hull, but the concept is very practical. You can easily build joinerwork to be as durable, stiff; strong and as structurally sound as wood, with about the same total weight. Bulkheads can be built with one quarter-inch thick plate (Type 5086) with 2 x 2 x 1/8 vertical stiffeners spaced twenty inches apart. One-eighth-inch plate can be use for the cabinetry with welded stiffeners spaced twenty inches on the vertical surfaces and ten inches on the horizontal surfaces. 2 x 2 x 1/8 stiffeners are adequate.

Attaching the aluminum to the hull is slightly more complicated than with other materials as glass overlay with epoxy resin will not adhere to aluminum. Resins only adhere to porous surfaces. Use the four-inch glass overlay to the hull and to the aluminum, using epoxy (sand both surfaces in preparation). After the resin has set drill one-quarter inch bolt holes through both glass and aluminum, spaced twelve inches apart. Install stainless steel bolts and washers with Loc-tite® on the threads. The cabin sole can also be one-quarter-inch thick aluminum with stiffeners spaced ten inches apart. It is secured to the glass hull in a similar manner as the bulkheads. Be sure to provide access hatches to all areas of the bilge. Vertical sections of aluminum joinerwork are welded to an aluminum cabin sole, but are secured to a glass fiber cabin sole with aluminum angles and bolts. Doors and drawers may be made of aluminum or purchased off the shelf in plastic.

CORE MATERIALS

There are many core materials on the market made from plastic, rigid foam, end grain balsa, sawdust with a glue binder and plastics in the shape of an open honeycomb form. All of these can be faced on both sides with any material, plastic, wood or metal. Probably the first use of lightweight core materials faced with sheet aluminum was for control surfaces on aircraft. The primary purpose of a core material is to provide a stiff structure with minimum weight. The amount of stiffness (resistance to bending) is determined by the thickness of the core and the thickness of the material on both sides.

Usually, the total thickness of facing material (skins) is calculated as 75 to 80 percent of the thickness of the solid glass fiber material used without a core. Thus, there is a considerable saving in weight. Care must be observed when the structure is subject to impact loads such as in a boat hull. Core material between a glass laminate (sandwich construction) is normally used only on hulls intended for racing where light weight is an asset. Average speed hulls usually have a solid glass laminate except in the deck and deckhouse structure.

The interior joinerwork can also be made from core materials faced with glass fiber and the outside surface can have any sort of decorative material. The edges are attached to the hull and cabin sole with glass overlay, as are the inside shelves. Counter tops can be surfaced with any durable material using contact cement. Where there are significant loads, such as on a berth, you must attach glass stiffeners to the underside, spaced ten inches apart. These can be 2 x 2 x 1/8 glass angles. Moldings and structural shapes made of glass fiber or other plastic composites are available on the market from many suppliers. Some of these are; Joseph Ryerson Inc., Charlotte, NC and CPI Plastics Group Ltd., Mississauga, Ontario, Canada. When using a core material for joinerwork, the components will have to be secured with glue, as screws and staples will not hold in most core materials. Make a test sample to insure the correct adhesive is used for the facing material on the core.

A FEW EXAMPLES

Figure 29 shows the construction of forward berths and shelves which also serve as hull stiffeners, as previously mentioned. The glass overlay to the hull on the outboard edges not only secures the joinerwork but is very important in the integrity of the entire boat. The bottom of the berth front is secured to a wood 2 x 2 cleat screwed to the cabin sole. Use stainless steel or silicon bronze fastenings throughout the boat. The top edge of the berth front can be capped with Formica® laminate or a plastic U-molding can be glued in place with contact cement. Note the top edge of the berth front extends about two inches above the berth flat so the mattress does not slide. This extension above the horizontal flat portion is typical for all counters and shelves to prevent articles from dropping to the floor. A centerline hatch in the cabin sole provides access to storage.

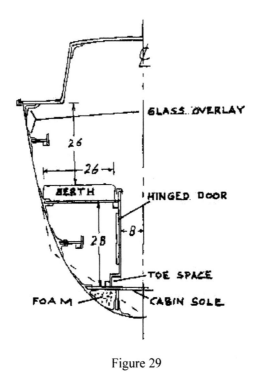

GLASS OVERLAY

26

26

BERTH

HINGED DOOR

28

8

TOE SPACE

FOAM

CABIN SOLE

Figure 29

Berth and shelf construction with a glass overlay to the hull.

Figure 30 shows typical construction at the galley and it is a continuation of Figure 29. There is not much description to add except a few notes on the icebox construction. Many boats that are used for just a few hours carry separate ice chests (coolers) for drinks and sandwiches and may also have an icebox built into the boat. Four to six inches of urethane foam insulation should be installed outside of a glass fiber, or glass lined, waterproof box. This can be used to hold ice or it may have a mechanical refrigeration system installed by the manufacturer. Of course, if you have AC electrical power, you may have an under counter or full-size refrigerator. If this is a box for a block of ice, there must be a shelf to keep food away from the wet ice. Water drains on the bottom of the box are almost useless as you have to drain to a bucket before disposing. If you drain to the bilges, they will smell forever of rotting food. It is easier to bail out the icebox with a pan and sponge. The icebox should have an opening only on the top (flush hatch) and be about 20" x 24" x 24" deep.

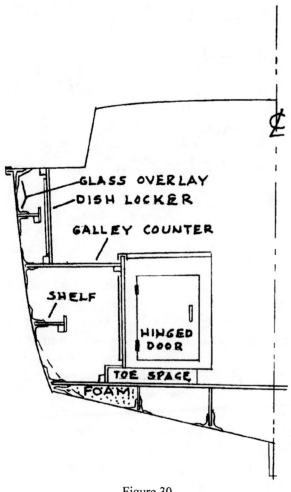

Figure 30

Typical galley construction.

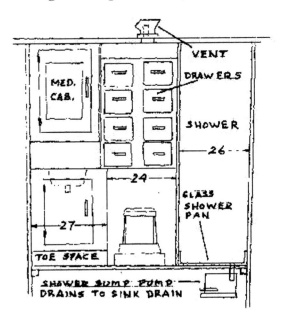

Figure 31

Typical head arrangement and construction.

Figure 31 shows a comfortable arrangement for a head and shower where the shower may be only 21 inches wide, if necessary. A water-trap cowl vent is necessary over the head or shower. Sometimes, an owner will want warm water for the shower, even when there is no hot water heater. This can be provided with a plastic removable or permanent tank located on the cabin top. This is painted black to absorb the heat of the sun and provides enough for some quick, warm showers. Many small drawers in the head are always appreciated, not only for the toilet articles for each person, but for first aid supplies and clean towels. Every available space on the bulkheads should have a towel bar or hooks.

Where bulkheads meet the underside of the deck, there should be glass overlay to secure them. Where this is not possible because of interference with the bulkhead covering, epoxy glue can be used. Where the joinerwork meets each bulkhead, screws and glue are used. The toilet should pump to a holding tank in the bilge, unless it is the self-contained type.

FINISHING THE INTERIOR

In Chapter Six I listed five alternatives for finishing the bulkheads and these suggestions also apply to the covering of the joinerwork. The five materials are:

1. Prime and paint. Edges may use a shaped wood molding, a plastic laminate glued to the edge or a plastic U-shaped molding.
2. Sand, seal and varnish if the underlying wood has an acceptable appearance. Varnish must be renewed every few years.
3. Cover with a plastic laminate.
4. Cover with a washable vinyl wall covering, usually with a texture.
5. Install fine wood paneling, which is an expensive alternative.

Figure 32 shows the varnished wood interior of a glass sailboat that is very well finished. Note the rounded wood corners of the lockers and drawers are made with a shaped molding. Curved corners are a sign of good workmanship. It is comfortable to lean into a rounded corner as the boat heels, but many bruises develop from banging into a sharp corner. Note the top edge of the molding extends above the horizontal surface to keep items from falling.

It is probably the least expensive to paint the boat interior, as it covers joinerwork that has a less than perfect surface. Figure 33 shows joinerwork being assembled in a glass sailboat where the cabinetry is made from pre-finished plywood, which is yet another option if you are careful not to scratch it during cutting and assembly.

Figure 32

Excellent use of wood is evident in this sailboat.

Figure 33

This shows the interior joinerwork in progress.

The finish on the overhead (underside of the deck) can use a variety of materials. If you have first laid pre-finished plywood or a decorative wood-faced plywood on the deck beams before laminating, the overhead may be completed or may just need varnishing. If the deck has been laminated with a core or with solid glass separate from the hull, the glass fiber may be painted or covered with carpeting glued to the glass with contact cement. One expensive solution is to glass 1 x 2 wood furring strips to the glass underside of the deck. Panels of decorative material of many types may then be screwed to the wood strips.

Rather than install dome lights on the overhead, it is much easier to put lamps on the bulkheads with the electrical wiring concealed behind a decorative wood or metal molding.

The inside of the hull is exposed above shelves, counters and berths and will have to be finished in some decorative manner. The overlay of the deck to the hull and the overlay of the shelves and berths to the hull leaves an area of visible roughness that some find objectionable. These areas of rough overlay can be sanded and covered with glass cloth that has a smooth, acceptable finish ready to paint. This is probably the least expensive solution to finishing the hullsides. Some builders have gone to the extreme of trowelling a mixture of resin and micro balloons onto the sanded surface of the hull interior. This is then sanded to a perfectly smooth finish. This requires a great amount of work and requires masking of all the previously installed joinerwork during sanding. As an alternative, carpeting may be glued to the glass hull with contact cement. This latter solution is used by many of the boat manufacturers in the USA in both powerboats and sailboats.

The hull surface is a compound curve and a flat material such as a plastic laminate, washable vinyl or wood paneling will not fit smoothly on these curves without cutting and splicing. Wood furring strips can be shaped and glassed to the inside of the hull so narrow strips of wood or other decorative material may be screwed to them. With a great amount of work, it is possible to install wood furring strips of different depths, so the inside edges are all on the same plane. In this case, flat panels may be screwed to the furring strips.

On the subject of finishing the interior, it cannot be overemphasized that the bottom edges and sides of all wood below the cabin sole be coated with resin to form a waterproof barrier. Use only exterior grade plywood made with waterproof glue and do not use flake board or particle board. Use 1 x 2 cleats on all corners and glue all parts with epoxy glue or a good waterproof glue. If a shelf will be used for heavy pots, it must be well supported.

SUMMARY

Building the interior is not difficult, but it does take a great amount of time to apply an acceptable decorative finish. The final detailing requires great patience, but it is an expression of fine workmanship. You have the bulkheads glassed in place to use as sides of each section of joinerwork. You then build each section according to your drawings, concentrating on one area at a time. Make sure the boat waterline is level, the bulkheads plumb (perpendicular to the waterline) and the cabin sole level. It will then be easier to get the horizontal counter tops level and the vertical pieces plumb. Remember the drawer slides (horizontal pieces) are screwed to beams supported at both ends. These beams must be perpendicular to the front of the cabinetry in both directions (horizontal and vertical) and they may or may not be level in the as-built condition. If these beams are not perpendicular, the drawer front will be at an angle to the cabinet front.

If you are a skilled carpenter, the joinerwork installation will not be a problem. Never use nails or staples on a boat as the twisting and vibration of the hull will loosen them. All wood work must be glued and screwed. A slow, careful approach will produce excellent results.

CHAPTER SIXTEEN
SAILBOATS

The glass laminations on the hull and deck of a sailboat are the same as a powerboat in the manner they are applied. Thickness will be different in the same length hull as the speed is different and the keel of the sailboat is usually much thicker in order to support the ballast and the compression load of the mast. These details and instructions should be noted on the drawings you have purchased. The sailboat will usually have a round bilge which will make the construction of a female mold more difficult as the mold surface will have to be made of smaller pieces in order to fit the compound curvature. This problem can be easily solved by using cardboard or other template material to fit the mold surface pieces before the expensive mold surface material is cut. Construction of a male mold or use of a sailboat shape with chines is no more difficult.

The wire rope rigging on a sailboat supports the mast and the headstay at the bow and provides a place to set the jib, forward of the mast. The rigging is secured to the hull by chainplates made of two-inch by sixteen-inch stainless steel bars. The thickness of the bars is the same as the maximum diameter of the wire rope rigging. Figure 34 shows the installation of these chainplates. There are normally eight chainplates on a hull: three on each side near the mast, one at the bow and one at the stern. Each chainplate has a hole at the top for the rigging toggle pin and the distance from the top of this hole to the top of the chainplate must be twice the wire diameter. As the pin wears on the hole, the hole becomes elongated and there must be sufficient metal area remaining so the chainplate will not break at the hole.

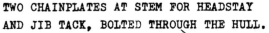

TWO CHAINPLATES AT STEM FOR HEADSTAY
AND JIB TACK, BOLTED THROUGH THE HULL.

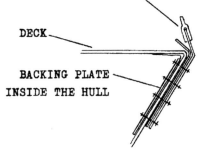

DECK

BACKING PLATE
INSIDE THE HULL

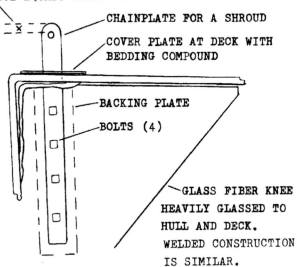

X DISTANCE EQUALS TWICE THE WIRE RIGGING DIAMETER.

CHAINPLATE FOR A SHROUD

COVER PLATE AT DECK WITH
BEDDING COMPOUND

BACKING PLATE

BOLTS (4)

GLASS FIBER KNEE
HEAVILY GLASSED TO
HULL AND DECK.
WELDED CONSTRUCTION
IS SIMILAR.

Figure 34

Proper attachment of sailboat chainplates.

At the stem, a padeye can be used for the jib tack instead of a second chainplate, but it must use four through bolts and a backing plate. At the sides, if the shroud chainplates cannot be bolted to a bulkhead, they must be bolted through a plywood knee with four, one-half inch bolts. The knee is heavily glassed to both the hull and the deck, after sanding the areas to be bonded.

The decision to have a sloop, cutter, yawl, ketch or schooner rig is just a matter of preference, but one mast is always less expensive than two. If you don't care for the type of sailboat rig you received with your drawings, you should ask the designer for changes. It is not correct to change the sail plan (rig) and keep the mast in the same position as the balance of the helm will be affected. This is a fairly complicated calculation but it involves the graphical center of the sail plan (Center Of Effort) and the graphical center of the underwater area of the hull (Center Of Lateral Plane). The objective of this calculation is to have a reasonable balance of the helm so the boat will not have a tendency to turn up into the wind nor turn off the wind direction. Changing the mast position, mast rake, size of the sails and wind strength will all change the balance of the helm. Many factors are taken into consideration when drawing a sail plan for a particular hull and they should be done by an experienced sailboat designer and not by an owner or a builder. Make sure all hardware and especially the mainsheet traveler is through bolted with backing plates.

The mast is normally stepped on (set on) the keel of the boat but it must have a wide area of support so the compression load of the mast is not concentrated in one spot. In a glass fiber hull the mast support (step) is easily made by cutting a piece of wood to fit the inside shape of the keel area, about two feet aft of where the mast will be located. Cover this with wax paper on the forward side to a depth of about one foot above the keel. Laminate scrap pieces of glass mat and woven roving with resin forward of the wood partition to a depth that produces a width at the top of about sixteen inches at the mast location. The top of this glass mast step should be level and it will taper to zero width about two feet forward of the mast location. Finish off the top of the mast step neatly with two layers of mat and woven roving extending over the hull at the sides.

Where the mast passes through the deck, the hole is somewhat larger than the mast and the edges of the hole at the deck must be sealed with resin to make it waterproof. Wood wedges or pieces of hard rubber are hammered into place between the mast and the deck edges. This is done firmly but not with a hard blow of the hammer. Since the mast moves from one side to the other as the boat tacks, these wedges or partners become loose and are held in place with a large stainless steel hose clamp. To keep water from entering around the mast, put a two-foot length of tire inner tube over the mast before it is stepped in the boat. Use hose clamps around the mast and around the partners.

The ballast in a sailboat may be thirty percent of the total displacement (weight) on a cruising boat and forty percent on a racing hull. However, on hulls over forty feet in length these ratios may be somewhat less. There are exceptions to this approximation of ballast ratio, but they usually occur on extreme racing hulls. The best advice is to follow the designer's calculations as they appear on the drawings. Do not change the drawings! The ballast is easily installed in a glass fiber boat inside the hull. Use round or rectangular lead pellets and avoid any other material. Pour some pellets in the bilges and cover with polyester resin and continue until the desired weight has been installed. The ends of the ballast can be formed with waxed plywood cut to the hull shape, in a similar manner as the mast step glass laminations.

The length and height of the ballast should follow the drawings, as the designer has spent hours calculating the best shape and position for the lead ballast. Not only is the ballast weight for increasing the ability to carry full sail, but it has a great effect on the trim of the boat. For this reason, you may see that the top edge of the ballast is not level but may be sloped down aft. This is because the designer wanted to get more ballast weight forward to keep the boat in level trim. The ballast not only must fit inside the compound shape of the hull, but it must be of the correct volume and in the proper location.

When the ballast installation is complete, cover it with two layers of mat and woven roving so water will not enter between the lead and the glass hull.

Recently, we have seen the use of port and starboard water tanks for ballast in some extreme racing hulls. This idea has sometimes spread to cruising boats with the thought that fresh water (instead of salt water) could be used so extra water can be carried and the weight used to improve stability in place of carrying so much lead. There is some slow thinking in this idea for cruising boats. The normal hull shape puts these port and starboard tanks well above the waterline where the weight is not effective for ballast. Ballast must be down in the keel. Of course, the water ballast is only effective if it is on the windward side of the hull. In times of a sudden squall or in an emergency, the last item of thought is to pump the water ballast from the lee side to the windward side. It may be very dangerous to have the leeward water tank full. Safe and sane operation tells us to stay with the proper amount of lead ballast in the keel and follow the designer's recommendations.

There is a great tendency to emulate the photos of the top racing sailboats and to install the mast and deck gear that they attempt to use. Not only is this a very expensive procedure, it is not necessary on a cruising boat. A cruising sailboat does not need two steering wheels, cross-linked sheet winches, a hydraulic boom vang, a light weight carbon fiber mast, run-fling backstays, a spinnaker pole or a reaching strut. Keep a cruising sailboat just what it is and concentrate on the ease of handling and the safety for the crew.

Buying a set of sails is like buying a suit, it is all a matter of personal preference. A cruising sailboat usually has sails made from Dacron sailcloth rather than one of the many more expensive materials. There are many experienced sailmakers that will provide an estimate of costs after looking at your sail plan. Many jibs have a clew (aft corner) aft of the mast when set and one or two feet of this overlap is fine for a cruising sailboat in moderate winds, but any more is not necessary and makes tacking that much harder. A large jib and mainsail are a deficit in winds over 14 knots, when sail area should be reduced on cruising boats.

A spinnaker always looks great and provides the extra sail area needed when sailing downwind on the slowest point of sailing. Some cruising sailboats with experienced skippers do fly a spinnaker when off the wind, but the sail should have about half the area as a spinnaker used for racing. That is, the height of the sail is about half the height of the mast. The spinnaker can be used very easily off the wind without a spinnaker pole and with the two sheets led to blocks at the widest beam of the boat.

There are some fine products on the market that make sail handling easier, such as roller reefing for both the jib and the mainsail. They allow rolling the sail around itself to reduce area in winds over 14 knots or when storing the sail after a cruise. If you will sail with just two people, it may be wise to investigate these various forms of roller reefing from different manufacturers. Rather than try to build your own wood mast, it is more practical to buy an aluminum mast, boom and rigging from a mast manufacturer. Any sailboat mast and rigging is expensive, but it will be necessary to have a very reliable and durable, low maintenance assembly.

CHAPTER SEVENTEEN
FULL FLOTATION

All boat owners are concerned with safety and especially keeping the boat from sinking after an accident. This chapter details the use of foam flotation material to accomplish that objective. In addition to foam flotation, it is important to keep water from spreading from the point of origin, whether a leaking hose fitting or a crack in the hull as a result of collision or grounding. Many watertight compartments are formed by having bulkheads made watertight to the hull from the keel to the sheer. Cabin soles are also watertight at the edges where they meet the hull and watertight hatches are used both in the bulkheads and in the cabin sole.

Flotation may be plastic foam, encapsulated balsa wood or other lightweight, non-porous material. Half of this material must be located on the hull sides in unballasted hulls as the boat may float upside down when flooded if all of the flotation material is located in the bottom of the hull. Usually, there is space available in both areas of the hull.

Recently, we have seen inflatable and rigid hull inflatable small boats with large diameter air tubes around the sheer (deck). These tubes provide full flotation so the boats are unsinkable. The same principle has been applied to large bulls and is a great step forward in boating safety. Figure 35 shows how this principle can be applied to boats of any length, with the additional advantage of having more room inside the boat. The hull sides are flared outboard from a point about two feet above the waterline so the beam at the deck is about four feet wider than usual. This allows the side deck walkway to be farther outboard, allowing a wider deckhouse or trunk cabin. Foam is installed under the side deck.

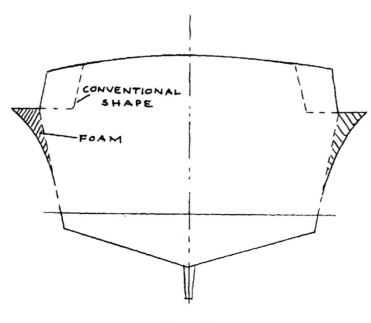

Figure 35

Powerboat section showing the use of a flared hull side to produce a wider beam, more interior space and an area for flotation.

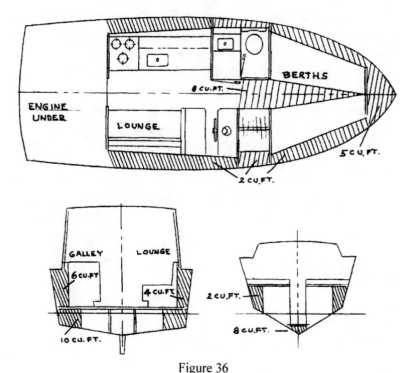

Figure 36

Example of full flotation layout.

It is not difficult to locate the amount of required foam in the hull, as shown in Figure 36. What is fairly difficult is determining the volume of the foam necessary for any particular boat. Experience has shown an average single engine boat without ballast may require thirty percent of the displacement volume in foam flotation to make it unsinkable. But, a twin engine boat with ballast and a large amount of steel equipment in the engineroom may require seventy percent of the displacement volume for full flotation. Thus, we cannot estimate the amount of foam required. We must make a detailed weight and volume calculation for each boat. The displacement volume is the total weight of the boat in pounds divided by the density of sea water; 64 pounds per cubic foot. This is the total volume that must be floated.

In a similar manner, the volume of every item in the boat is determined by dividing the weight of that item by the density of the material with which it is made. The total of all these items in the boat is subtracted from the boat displacement volume to find the required volume of flotation material. These calculations are based on the scientific law of flotation that says a floating body displaces its own weight of water. In other words, each item is buoyed up by the weight of water of the same volume as the item.

DENSITIES OF A FEW BOAT MATERIALS	
ITEMS	LBS/Ft^3
Aluminum	165
Bronze	480-520
Canned Food (12 oz)	50
Sodas in Aluminum Cans	42
Copper	550
Glass Fiber	96
Gasoline	46
Diesel Fuel	53
Lead	700
Oak	52
Fir Plywood	36
Steel	490
Window Glass	160
Fresh Water	62.4
Sea Water	64

The designer calculates the weight of every item in the boat in order to determine what the boat will weigh (displacement) before he draws the lines of the hull. This weight list is then expanded to find the total volume of the items in the boat. This takes some time, but it is within your capabilities to find out how much foam you will need.

For example, if an engine weighs 980 pounds, we assume it is all steel and divide by 490 pounds per cubic foot. This results in a volume of two cubic feet that will be subtracted from the displacement volume, together with the volume of all other items in the boat. If the boat weighs 15,000 pounds, we divide by 64 pounds per cubic foot of sea water to arrive at a volume of 234.375 cubic feet.

The flotation material must be impervious to salt water and capable of being cut into shapes or poured into the small spaces in the bottom and sides of the hull. Urethane foam and PVC foam are commonly available. Spaces outboard of the engine girders and under the cabin sole are normally unused and are ideal for the foam flotation.

CHAPTER EIGHTEEN
STABILITY

Good stability is defined as the ability of a boat to return to the upright position after heeling over from the force of wind or wave. This ability to level out depends on a low center of gravity of all the weights in the boat and the positive influence of a wide beam. Sailboats with ballast normally have good stability because the ballast weight counteracts the heeling energy of the wind on the sails. Sailboats without ballast are inherently unstable and will capsize if the crew is not alert. Smaller boats of all types are not usually stable as the weight of people, especially when standing, raises the total center of gravity to a point where there is an unsafe situation. This becomes obvious in a narrow, slender hull, such as a canoe, where it is only the skill of the crew that keeps it upright.

Powerboats usually do not have ballast as the generous beam and the somewhat rectangular sectional shape provide adequate hull stability. The center of gravity on normal recreational powerboats is relatively low, which is always desirable. However, this may change if there is a 'tuna tower" for visibility when sport fishing or when there is a crane and tender on the foredeck. Commercial fishing boats sometimes have stability problems if there are steel masts, an A-frame, heavy blocks and wire rope rigging. All of these contribute to a high center of gravity which is made increasingly worse if ice forms during winter fishing.

If a boat rolls easily, it is called "tender," which may or may not indicate inadequate stability. A round bilge hull will roll easier than a V-bottom hull with a chine. When in the trough of a wave, any hull will roll to the point of being uncomfortable and an experienced skipper will change course or increase speed to stay out of the trough.

The designer goes through some long and tedious calculations for stability which determine both the amount of positive stability and the extent of heel angle where this positive stability exists. This latter point is extremely important as we must know how far the hull can be rolled before it will not return to the upright position. This heel angle of zero stability varies widely with the type of hull and the loading in the hull. It may be 45 degrees in a multihull, 65 degrees in an average cruising powerboat without ballast and 125 degrees in a ballasted sailboat. A sailboat may get knocked down with the top of the mast in the water and thus the heel angle of zero stability must be at least 110 degrees. The stability calculations are always different even with hulls of the same type and length. If you question the stability of your boat, the best answers can only be provided by the designer.

If an owner feels his boat rolls excessively, there are some remedial installations that can be made. First, install a centerline keel if there is not one on the hull. This will reduce rolling and protect the propeller at the same time. This is accomplished by epoxy gluing a solid glass sheet or foam core of one-quarter to three-quarter inch thickness to the hull centerline. Laminate solid glass to both sides of this core using alternating layers of mat and woven roving with either polyester or epoxy resin, overlapping the hull bottom at least six inches. It is always difficult to adhere glass to the vertical and overhead surfaces and it must be held in position until the initial set is achieved by using wood sticks with wax paper on the end. Resin will become warm in temperature and tend to drain away from the glass material. It will be necessary to continually roll the material and resin together during the first ten to twenty minutes of application. The thickness of the laminate should be at least one-quarter inch on the sides of the keel and hull bottom, and one inch on the bottom of the keel. If you go aground frequently, as many of us do, you may want a cypress wood wear strip epoxy glued to the bottom of the glass keel. Do not consider bilge keels as they are usually not effective.

If the boat has a keel and still rolls too much, try temporary lead blocks (pigs) on the inside of the hull bottom for ballast. Usually five percent of the boat weight (displacement) will be sufficient. If this helps the problem, glass the lead to the hull to make it permanent. If there is very little change in the motion of the boat with the temporary ballast, you might try installing glass angles on the sides of the glass keel, so the keel section shape looks like an inverted letter "T." In hulls of other materials you would use steel or aluminum angles welded to the keel, but on a glass hull you should use solid glass fiber plates. These extend about six inches on both sides on the bottom of the keel and are tapered forward to zero width at the bow. The thickness of these solid glass fiber plates can be one-quarter inch on boats under thirty feet in length and one-half inch thickness on longer hulls.

When starting a long cruise, load all the groceries in the bottom of the hull and do not carry heavy loads on deck. If extra fuel is carried on deck, it should be no more than fifty gallons and it must be well secured from any movement. High weights on the deck give a high center of gravity and contribute to poor stability. All of these discussions on stability assume there are no openings where water can enter the hull. There should be no opening ports or vents in the side of the hull and all ports in the cabin side should be closed when cruising in open water. The entrance from the deck to the hull should be close to the boat centerline so that excessive rolling does not allow water to enter.

You can check the range of positive stability in your unballasted powerboat of under 35 feet in length if you are willing to go to a great deal of effort and expense. But, if you are operating off offshore, it is very reassuring to know the limits of your boat. Lead or steel weights can be carefully weighed and secured to the side deck amidships. Lines to cleats may be sufficient to hold the weights in place. Weights are added until the rail (sheer) amidships is in the water and if possible, the water level is at the cabin side. This demonstrates the heeling ability of the boat in a positive manner. If at any time the boat tends to heel more easily or heels more with just the body weight, further weights should not be added as there is a danger of capsizing. Proceed at you own risk! No definitive measurements are taken, but an inclinometer (pendulum) will indicate the maximum heel angle achieved. The amount of weight put on one side of the deck and its distance from the centerline would be of great interest to the designer in reaffirming his stability calculations.

Some sailboats under thirty feet have been heeled over until the top of the mast is in the water. This was done to check the stability and was accomplished by having a crane pull down from the masthead. This also checks the soundness of the wire rope rigging that supports the mast. You have possibly heard of the inclining test performed on all ships by heeling the ships with weights placed on one rail. This is done to only four or five degrees of heel 'to check the designer's calculations. This small angle of heel is noteworthy on ships but is of no value with the types of small boats discussed herein.

CHAPTER NINETEEN
CATAMARANS

I have primarily discussed monohulls as that is the area of greatest demand, but recently there has been an increase in multihulls on the water, especially with passenger boats. The glass fiber laminate and form of construction is no different for catamarans, but the hull shape and some details are very unique and are worth mentioning.

The primary advantage of the catamaran is the wide deck space that opens many possibilities for new arrangements in both cruising boats and commercial vessels. The overall beam of a catamaran should be about forty to fifty percent of the overall boat length in order to make best use of the boat type. A narrow beam catamaran is a waste of time and effort. The catamaran has a great resistance to rolling which is much appreciated by the crew and is mainly why the catamaran is desired. The minimum width between the inside of the hulls should be twenty percent of the overall length and the minimum height of the deck above the water should be ten percent of the overall length. These dimensions ensure a minimum of pounding when the boat proceeds into a head sea.

The primary disadvantage of the catamaran hull is that it requires a wider docking space. Since there are two hulls to build and there is more hull surface than a monohull, the catamaran is more expensive to build. In addition to the possibility of pounding if the spacing between hulls is not sufficient, a sailing catamaran will capsize if it is heeled over forty-five degrees without ballast. The skill of the crew is extremely important.

The exterior profile styling of the catamaran should not be any less attractive than that of a monohull, as shown in Figure 37.

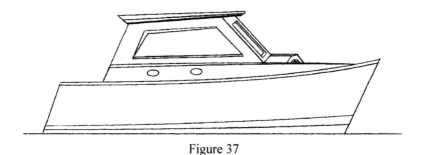

Figure 37

An example of catamaran styling.

The height and shape of the sheer (deck at side) is located to produce a pleasing balance between the height of the hull and the height of the deck house. Very often it is necessary to have the height of the hull higher than the sheer in order to get full headroom inside the hull. This is accomplished by designing a seat all around the deck house and the full length of each hull. There is a side deck about sixteen inches inside the sheer and then the seat about eighteen inches wide before meeting the outside of the cabin side.

Figure 38 shows some of the shapes that can be used for a catamaran hull and the final decision is usually based on the interior space requirements. The hulls are connected by beams covered both top and bottom with the deck material. Not only do these beams support the deck and the deck house over it, but they are the primary structural support for the hulls and must be extremely well built. The designer determines the size and material of the beams by assuming one hull and all of the deck superstructure are cantilevered without support from the other hull that is supported. This is equivalent to the momentary condition when one hull is supported by the crest of a wave and the other hull is hanging in air over the trough of a wave. Because of headroom considerations in each hull, the height of the deck beams usually cannot be bolted to bulkheads inside the hulls. The beams are normally securely bolted and glassed to athwartships framing on the inboard sides of each hull. These joints are the most important in the boat.

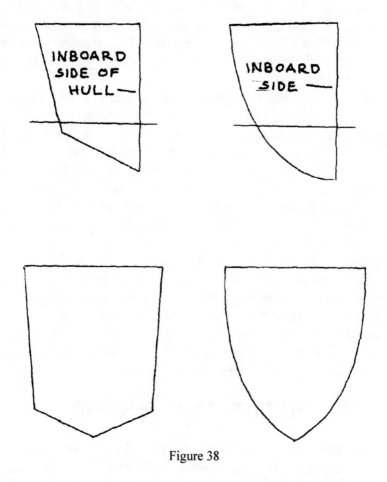

Figure 38

Examples of catamaran sectional hull shapes.

Construction of catamarans may be accomplished in either of two procedures. Usually, the frames are made from the loft in the usual manner, with the deck beams bolted to the side frames for both hulls. This ensures a very sound structure and the glass fiber laminations can proceed using the same technique as for a monohull. It is important to have the hull laminations continue in a smooth transition to the bottom of the deck, usually with a large radius where the hull side meets the bottom of the deck. Whether the frames are made from wood or from solid glass sheets, they are overlaid to the bottom of the deck with heavy glass laminations. The sizes of these frames and the thickness of the hull and deck are determined by the designer on your drawings.

It is possible to construct the catamaran if the hulls are laminated separately and then attached by bolting and glassing beams to the framing on the inboard sides of each hull. Both hulls must be set in cradles and very carefully aligned so each hull is in the same fore-and-aft position, the centerlines are parallel and to be certain the hulls are not tilted. The beams that form the deck structure between the hulls may be bought as glass fiber I-beams or fabricated from flat glass fiber sheets overlaid to the top and bottom deck surfaces. After one deck surface is glassed to the deck beams, it may be difficult to overlay the other surface to these beams. This overlay may be accomplished by working from both hulls and putting the glass material in place with the help of rods or wood sticks that have wax paper on the ends. You may only have four inches of opening in which to work, but careful and patient glass overlay will produce a good structural bond.

CATAMARAN INTERIORS

The construction of the hulls and interior are similar to that of a monohull as there must be bulkheads and adequate framing glassed to the hull according to the drawings. The hulls are designed as narrow as possible in a catamaran in order to achieve minimum resistance but they must have sufficient interior width to have adequate berth width and an amply wide walking space past the berths.

The engines are aft in each hull with space for batteries, generators, fuel and water tanks. The heads are usually in the hulls with the galley either in the hull or on deck. A trunk cabin forward of the deck house may conceal a double bed installed athwartships with only sitting headroom. Ladders must be provided to access the hulls from the deck. In a sailing catamaran, centerboards may be installed in watertight trunks wherever it is most convenient and not necessarily on the hull centerlines. A keel on each hull is desirable to protect the propellers and a cypress wear strip at the bottom of the keels protects the glass fiber when aground

One of the fine advantages of a catamaran is the privacy found with two hulls. If the interior is fitted out with berths and heads in each hull, people can be completely separate from one another in the sleeping accommodations. If you have the interior for just one family or for living aboard, you might have the berths in one hull and an office and working space in the other. The deck area is usually reserved for the galley and dining table, keeping the forward portion for the helm and electronics. The convenience of having the helm and charts out of the weather is what the experienced owner always chooses, no matter what type of hull is selected.

Building A Fiberglass Boat by Arthur Edmunds

154

CHAPTER TWENTY
EXTRA STRENGTH IN YOUR GLASS HULL

THE KEEL

The designer will show the laminate thickness on the drawings and the keel area will always be the thickest. The reason for this is the stress imposed when the boat is bouncing on a trailer or when the boatyard sets the hull on only two keel blocks. The side supports are usually set loosely to keep the boat from tilting to one side.

For example, if a boat weighs 6000 pounds and is set on two keel blocks where the bearing area is only two inches in width, the load is 3000 pounds on each keel area. The compressive strength of a normal glass laminate is ten thousand pounds per square inch and we use a factor of safety of four. The required thickness of the keel is 4 x 3000 divided by 10000 x 2 which equals 0.6 inches. If you have any question of how much laminate you have put into the keel, use all the scrap pieces left in the shop.

ACCIDENTAL COLLISION

The designer calculates the laminate thickness based on normal operating stress the boat is expected to see. The designer cannot be responsible for unusual situations where the hull is pushed into a rock or another boat. In a cruising boat, you may want to reinforce the most vulnerable areas.

I have discussed the placement of foam flotation at the bow both above and below the waterline where cracks are usually found. In addition, it is a good idea to continue the thickness of the keel (noted above) throughout the boat's centerline from stem to stern. This additional thickness overlaps the hull about six inches on both sides of the centerline.

When a glass hull hits a dock amidships or is rammed from the side, there is no guarantee the glass will not crack. The loads are difficult to estimate and it is not practical to increase the thickness of the entire hull to anticipate some accident in the future. This example is an excellent reason for having a strong laminate at the joint of the deck to the hull, as I have previously discussed. In all cases of accident, one of the best preventative measures is to make sure there are adequate hull stiffeners spaced not more than twenty inches apart. Before a glass hull cracks, it will have to bend (flex) to the point of failure. If we can prevent flexing, we will usually prevent hull cracks.

THE DECK HOUSE

In a full gale or with extreme rolling of the boat, windows may break in the deck house or the house may be completely swept off the hull. This occurs when the house is set on the deck without adequate support to the hull. In a glass fiber hull, the glass deck house sides must be glassed (overlaid) to the underside of the deck. This forms a continuous overlay to the reinforcement of the deck and hull joint. Vertical glass framing is a necessity in the deck house to prevent any lateral movement.

In a small boat where there is no intrusion with accommodations below decks -- as on a commercial fishing boat -- it may be the easiest and strongest installation to have the house framing extend down to the hull bottom. This is illustrated in Figure 39. The bottom of the glass deck house framing is glassed to the hull and forms a very stiff structure for both the house and the side decks.

STRONGER THROUGH HULL FITTINGS

When installing a through hull fitting and seacock or a rudder port, it is a sign of good construction to increase the thickness of the hull at these openings. This is accomplished by laminating an extra eighth of an inch of glass, over an area twelve inches square around the hole. Glass mat and woven roving can be used with a finishing layer of glass cloth to make the surface smoother.

The stress of turning the rudder sometimes puts a side load on the rudder tube and the glass laminate receives this load on a continual basis. Extra laminate in areas of stress is always recommended.

Recent years have seen many articles in the magazines about glass hull building techniques that aim to produce a lighter hull. Usually, these articles concern only racing hulls and the need for a lighter hull in cruising boats never becomes a reality.

We have previously mentioned the installation of the propeller shaft log (stuffing box) that prevents water from entering the hull. This is obviously the largest through hull fitting in the boat and as such must be strongly reinforced with laminate the same as the hull bottom thickness. It is good practice to extend this overlay to the longitudinal engine girders and the extra transverse framing that supports the hull bottom in the area of the engineroom.

CHAPTER TWENTY ONE
IMPORTANT CONSTRUCTION DETAILS

HULL AND LAMINATE

1. Laminating glass fiber material to make a boat hull depends entirely on the skill of the person doing the laminating. The resulting quality of the hull can only be assured if the laminator is very careful to use the correct material and resin at the proper temperatures and to roll the resin into the glass so that there is a high ratio of glass to resin.

2. If you purchase a bare hull instead of fabricating one yourself, be sure to get as much information as you can from the seller and from other owners who have built from this hull. Their experiences are invaluable and you will avoid many mistakes if you listen carefully to the problems they have encountered. The seller of the hull should show you that the laminate consists of alternating layers of glass mat and woven roving. A piece of equipment known as a chopper gun should never be used on boats as it produces an all-mat laminate with little structural strength.

3. When you are lofting the hull lines before you start construction, take the time to have each line accurately drawn full size, so that it accurately reflects the hull shape that the designer intended. Make sure that you understand every line. The accuracy of the subsequent templates will depend upon the care that you take in drawing the hull lines.

4. If the Table Of Offsets is made to the outside of the hull, your loft of the hull lines will also be to the outside of the hull. When you scribe the templates for the mold frames you must subtract the hull thickness at one particular area so that the outside of the mold frames shows the inside of the glass hull. Remember that the hull thickness will vary from the hull sides to the hull bottom and to the keel. This procedure is only for the method that uses the male plug, over which the hull will be laminated.

When you laminate the hull inside a female mold surface, the mold frames are outside the hull, outside the mold battens and outside the mold surface. The inside of the mold surface is the outside of the hull. When lofting, the mold surface thickness and the batten thickness will have to be subtracted from the hull templates in order to get the proper dimensions for the inside of the mold frames.

5. After the mold frames are set into position, take the time to double check that they are in the correct longitudinal and transverse positions. Use the long batten over all of the outside edges of the mold frames to make sure that they are describing a fair, smooth hull surface.

6. The glass material should be kept covered in the original shipping covering as high humidity will affect the strength of the laminate. The resin should be purchased in small containers as it has a shelf life of about three months. In addition, the resin is highly flammable and it should be stored in an outside locker, separate from any other material.

7. The temperature of the laminating area should be between 65 and 85 degrees for the proper cure of the resin to glass bond. At the end of the laminating day, use a peel ply (Veil Cloth) to insure that the subsequent chemical bonding of the glass to resin will be structurally sound.

8. When sanding the outside of the laminate produced on a male plug, sand only on the micro balloons and never on the glass laminate itself Check the smoothness of the laminate with the long batten and fill the low areas with micro balloons. These areas then become high spots that can be sanded.

Continue over all the hull surface.

9. Study both the male plug and female mold methods before proceeding with the mold construction. Both methods can be used for more than one identical hull, but the female mold procedure will require little, if any, sanding of the outside of the hull surface.

10. With both mold methods, use a wood extension of the mold surface at the sheer (waxed), so that the laminate can be rolled tightly in a flat sheet. At the sheer (deck) the laminate has a tendency to splay out into an unmanageable clump of glass and resin.

11. Whenever the bulkheads or joinerwork are overlaid with glass to the hull (secondary bonding), make sure the hull and bulkhead areas are sanded clean to a width of six inches. These areas cause some concern as the hull ages over the years. The hull is subject to twisting and bending as it moves through a seaway and these secondary bonds may loosen if they are not carefully made when the boat is new.

12. Follow the instructions on your drawings carefully when installing the hull stiffeners. If possible, it is most efficient to have these stiffeners also supporting the joinerwork inside the boat. Sand the hull before using glass overlay on these stiffeners.

13. Make sure that there are hatches in the cabin sole to provide access to all through hull fittings, bilge pumps and valves on the tanks. All areas of the bilges should be visible for inspection, except where foam flotation is installed. In the engineroom, make sure you can reach the propeller shaft stuffing box. Hatches must be aft to provide access to the rudders.

14. It is always prudent to install a keel to protect the propellers when aground. The keel will also make steering easier in a seaway, especially when using an autopilot. A cypress wood wear strip can be epoxy glued to the bottom of the keel in order to protect the glass laminate.

15. It is not good design to have opening portlights or engineroorn vents in the sides of the hull. Ventilation should be

provided from ducts or water-trap vents installed on the deck. A ventilation box may be installed just forward of the deck house or windshield to serve two or three compartments. It is probably most necessary to have ventilation in the boat when the boat is at the dock, as this is where it is most of the time. Underway, the movement of the boat provides good air flow.

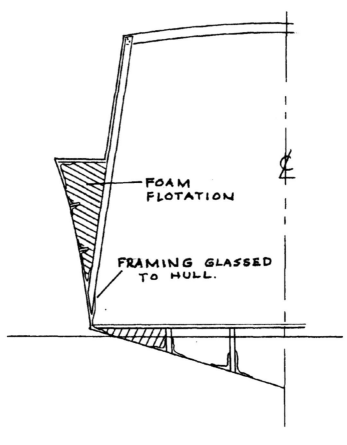

Figure 39

An example of solid construction of deck house framing.

162

THE DECK

1. Make sure a nonskid finish is applied. This can be in the form of paint with sand or a special plastic sheet that is glued to the glass deck.

2. The glass overlay of the deck edge to the hull at the sheer must be one of the strongest areas of the hull. Use a thick glass laminate that extends to six inches on both the hull and deck.

3. All hatches on deck and doors, must have screens and strong locks. The various manufacturers usually provide these when ordering a hatch that is specifically made for boats. It is very time consuming to make the hatches in your own shop and it is usually money well spent to order from the manufacturers.

4. It is extremely important that all deck hardware be through bolted to the deck using large backing plates. Under the deck, these backing plates are made from one-quarter inch thick aluminum plate with an area twice the width and twice the length of the bolt hole spacing.

5. The boat must be prepared for any emergency, including man overboard and recovering any equipment that might be lost at sea, such as fire extinguishers, life jackets (PFD), first-aid material and bilge pumps. It is important to have a swim platform on the stem or a permanently installed boarding ladder. The platform on the transom is useful for swimming from the boat or when boarding fish too large for a hand net.

6. The anchor can easily bang into the hull and scratch the paint. This can be avoided by installing an anchor platform at the bow. The platform has a roller to guide the anchor line and extends 24 to 40 inches forward of the stem. Stainless steel pipe can be bent into a "U" shape for this platform and is bolted through the hull with welded flanges, aft.

7. Lifelines, or a handrail, should be all around the deck with the top about 33 to 40 inches high. Two lower, horizontal lifelines should be equally spaced to keep people from rolling overboard in a sea way. The bottom of the vertical posts

(stanchions) have flanges bolted through the deck with large backing plates.

8. When the bolt holes are drilled for deck hardware to be through bolted, the edges of the bolt holes must be sealed with resin. If water seeps into the glass laminate, separation of the glass plies and delamination may occur. Bedding compound must be used when bolting all hardware to prevent this water penetration. The backing plates under the deck allow the bolts to be tightened securely so the bedding compound is well distributed and a watertight seal is formed.

9. When you install a fishing chair in the aft fishing cockpit, it not only must be through bolted to the deck, but there must be a post under the deck to support the load. This post may be a wood 3 x 3 or a three-inch diameter glass pipe with one-quarter inch wall thickness. The post is glassed to the underside of the deck and to a transverse frame at the bottom of the hull. Use a heavy laminate for the overlay.

THE ENGINE ROOM

1. Great care must be taken when installing the engine, shaft, propeller strut, rudder and steering system. Any error in this drive train will prevent proper operation. All fittings must be through bolted with backing plates. The laminate around the shaft tube and stuffing box (water seal) should be the same thickness as the bottom of the hull. The engine mounts are different on most engines and templates must be made to fabricate the steel assembly bolted to the engine girders. The spacing of the glass transverse frames in the engine room is half that in the remainder of the hull. Glass plate brackets are installed from the top of these frames to the top of the engine girders.

2. Do not use integral tanks in a glass fiber hull. The hull will flex in a seaway and the tank sides will come loose from the hull. There are many good marine tank manufacturers and their advice should be followed. They can be contacted through your local boat yard or from ads.

3. Do not locate fuel or water tanks at the stern or bow of the boat. The boat will always be out of trim, except when they are empty and useless, The tanks should be located close to the middle of the boat so trim is not affected. Usually, water tanks can be put on the boat centerline, just above the keel. Fuel tanks can be placed in the engine room, outboard of the engines. If the beam will not permit this location, the bilges on the boat centerline can be used, with the tanks set end to end, close to the middle of the boat. All tanks must be tested to a minimum of five psi.

4. When installing a through hull fitting, use extra glass laminate at this location and seal the edges of the hole with resin. Many holes through the hull can be eliminated by installing a sea chest where one hole in the hull provides sea water for cooling of all the equipment.

5. The exhaust system has to be gas tight and well supported throughout its length. In a wet exhaust, the highest point of the system must be near the engine so water will not enter the aft outlet and proceed forward to the engine. Beware of leaks where the exhaust leaves the engine.

6. Do not use wire nuts on any part of the electrical wiring. Use only crimped or soldered connectors.

7. Even though a glass fiber hull should be absolutely watertight, without leaks at any fitting, you have to be prepared for emergencies. For safety, install 12 VDC bilge pumps in the bilge with one between each pair of bulkheads. The pumps should have strainers and be accessible through hatches installed in the cabin sole.

8. The bulkheads at both ends of the engine room should be watertight from the rest of the boat. If there is a water leak, it may not be noticed immediately. It should be contained in one area and not allowed to flow to other parts of the hull.

9. Do not use reducing elbows in any sea water inlet piping. Grass can accumulate in the elbows and prevent water flow even before the sea water strainer. If there is a difference in pipe size, use a reducing fitting designed only to be used in a

straight section of piping.

JOINERWORK

1. It is wise to make a cardboard model of the interior, after the bulkheads have been installed. You can use old shipping boxes, cut, folded, glued and taped in place to the exact dimensions shown on your drawings. In this manner, you can see problems that may occur, and where the interior can be glassed to the hull and bulkheads.

2. Plan the glass overlay to the hull so a hull stiffener will be formed and additional framing may not be required. All joinerwork must be secured to the hull, bulkheads and the cabin sole.

3. If the bulkheads are made of wood, all areas must be coated with resin so water will not rot or delaminate the wood below the level of the cabin sole.

4. Flotation material, carefully calculated, can be installed outboard of the joinerwork or in the hull bottom to make the boat unsinkable. This is a great safety feature and the boat designer should be contacted to obtain the correct amount of material required. The flotation material, or watertight void spaces, can be fixed in place with glass overlay.

5. Careful planning must be given to the head, even though this is where you spend the least amount of time. Just as in your house, everything must be provided for maximum convenience and cleanliness. The traditional medicine cabinet becomes inconvenient when the boat rolls or there are more than three people on board. It is a great help to have as many small drawers as possible so each person has a place for toilet articles.

6. Most areas of the USA require the head to be discharged to a shore side sanitary drain facility. If the head has an overboard discharge only for use in the open ocean, it must have a siphon break to prevent accidental flow of sea water into the head.

7. The joinerwork should be installed in the most

professional manner possible as this determines the future value of the boat and is a reflection on the abilities of the builder. Not only does the finish of the interior show fine workmanship, but there are two items that show careful attention to detail. Where any part of the vertical faces of the joinerwork meet the cabin sole, there should be a three-inch toe space so a person can comfortably stand close to the cabinetry. Also, where there is a corner in the joinerwork close to the centerline passageway, it should be a round corner rather than a square corner. This rounded corner can be made from laminated wood or from plastic foam covered with glass overlay, depending on the type of final finish that will be applied. A great amount of patience and working hours are required to achieve a fine interior. Carpeting may be acceptable on the sole and hull sides, but it does not look good when applied to the vertical surfaces of the joinerwork.

8. Do not install a heater in the cabin that uses an open flame without having an outside air vent to prevent carbon monoxide from causing death to the crew. If you purchase a gas, kerosene, diesel fuel, wood or coal heater, be sure to follow the manufacturer's instruction for installation of the air vent.

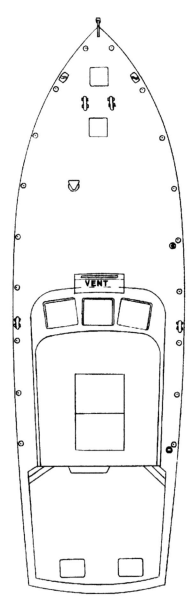

Figure 40

This deck plan shows the layout of all components on deck.

APPENDIX ONE
LIST OF ILLUSTRATIONS

APPENDIX TWO
OTHER HELPFUL BOOKS

The following list of books, published by Bristol Fashion Publications, will help you understand the many facets of boat construction and repair. Before you decide to take on a new boat building project or a major renovation project, it would be wise to read and understand all the information you can acquire.

Boat Repair Made Easy Haul Out
Written By John P. Kaufman

Boat Repair Made Easy Finishes
Written By John P. Kaufman

Boat Repair Made Easy Systems
Written By John P. Kaufman

Boat Repair Made Easy Engines
Written By John P. Kaufman

Designing Power & Sail
Written By Arthur Edmunds

APPENDIX THREE
SUPPLIERS AND MANUFACTURERS

The following list of Suppliers and Manufacturers does not constitute a complete directory of all the fine manufacturers and suppliers available throughout the country. This in no way indicates you should only deal with these companies; as always ask your friends for their recommendations. In most cases you will not be disappointed following their guidance.

SUPPLIERS

Boat/US: Boat Supplies, 800-937-2628, 880 S Pickett St. Alexandria, VA 22304

Defender: Boat Supplies, 800-628-8225, P O Box 820 New Rochelle, NY 10802-0820

Diesel Engineering & Marine Services: Engine repair and parts, 800-742-1169, P O Box 276, Port Salerno, FL 34992

Depco Pump Co: Pump supplies and parts, 813-446-1656, 1227 S Linoln Ave., Clearwater, FL 34616

E & B Discount Marine: Boat Supplies, 800-262-8464, P O Box 3138, Edison, NJ 08818-3138

Home Depot: Tools/Supplies, Located in most cities throughout the country. Look in local phone book.

Jamestown Distributors: Boat Building/Repairing Supplies, 800-423-0030, 28 Narragansett Ave., P O Box 348, Jamestown, RI 02835

Marine Propulsion: Genset & Transmission Repair, 561-283-6486, 3201 S. E. Railroad Ave., Stuart, FL 34997

West Marine: Boat Supplies, 800-538-0775, P O Box 50050, Watsonville, CA 95077-5050

MANUFACTURERS

AFI: Teak accessories, shelving and organizers. 2655 Napa Valley Corporate Dr., Napa, CA 94558.

Alaska Diesel Electric: Engines, 206-789-3880, 4420 14 Ave. N.W., Seattle, WA 98107-0543

Balmar: Alternators and Controls, 902 N.W. Ballard Way, Seattle, WA 98107

Camping World, RV Furnishings & Accessories, 800-893-1923, Three Springs Rd., Bowling Green, KY 42102.

Caterpillar: Engines, 800-447-4986, 2001 Ruppman Plaza, Peoria, IL 61614

Cummings Marine: Engines, 803-745-1171, 4500 Leeds Ave., Suite 301, Charleston, SC 29405

Datamarine International, Inc.: Electronics Instruments, 508-563-7151, 53 Portside Drive, Pocasset, MA 02559

Davis Instruments: Navigation Instruments and Marine Accessories, 415-732-9229, 3465 Diablo Ave., Hayward, CA 94545

Daytona Marine Engine Corp.: Engines, 904-676-1140, 1815 N. U. S. 1, Ormond Beach, FL 32174

Detroit Diesel: Engines, 313-592-5000, 13400 Outer Drive W., Detroit, MI 48239

Deutz MWM/KHD Canada: Engines, 514-335-3150, 4420 Garand, Ville St. Laurent, Quebec, Canada H4R 2A3

Dometic: galley Equipment, 219-294-2511, fax 912-293-9686, P O Box 490, Elkhart, IN 46515

Espar Heater Systems: Cabin Heaters, 416-670-0960, 6435 Kestrel Road, Mississauga, Ontario, Canada L5T 128

Fastening Solutions, Inc.: Heavy-Duty Grips, 800-232-7836, fax 818-997-1371, E-mail fastening@earthlink.net, Web site www.Fasteningsolutions.com, 15230 Burbank

Blvd., Suite 106, Van Nuys, CA 91411.

Fireboy Halon Systems Division-Convenience Marine Products, Inc.: Fire Suppression Equipment, 616-454-8337, P O Box 152, Grand Rapids, MI 49501

Furuno USA Inc.: Electronics, 415-873-4421, P O Box 2343, South San Fransico, CA 94083

Galley Maid Marine Products, Inc.: Galley, Water Supply and Waste, 407-848-8696, 4348 Westroads Drive, West Palm Beach, FL 33407

General Electric Company, Appliance Park, Louisville, KY 40225.

Get Organized: Storage Space Products, 800-803-9400, 600 Cedar Hollow Rd., Paoli, PA 19301, Web site www.getorginc.com.

Gougeon Brothers, Inc.: West System Epoxy, 517-684-7286, PO Box 908, Bay City, MI 48707

Hammacher Schlemmer & Company: Unusual Products, 212 W. Superior, Chicago, IL 60610.

Heart Interface Corp.: Inverters, Chargers, Monitors, Electrical, 1-800-446-6180, 21440 68th Ave. S., Kent, WA 98032

Hubbell Wiring Device Division, Hubbell Inc.: Electrical products, 203-337-3348, P O Box 3999, Bridgeport, CT 06605

Icom America, Inc.: Electronics, 206-454-8155, 2380 116th Ave. NE, Bellevue, WA 98004

InterCon Marketing Inc., Lighting and Boat Accessories, 1121 Lewis Ave., Sarasota, FL 34237. Web site www.interconmktg.com. E-mail icmmktg@gte.net.

Interlux Paints: Varnish, Paint, Coatings, 908-964-2285, 2270 Morris Ave, Union, NJ 07083

Jenn-Air Company: Cooktop and Ranges, 3035 Shadeland, Indianapolis IN 46226.

Lister-Petter, Ltd: Engines, 913-764-3512, 815 E. 56 Highway, Olathe, KS 66061

MAN Marine Engines: Engines, 954-771-9092, 6555 NW 9th Ave., Suite 306, Ft. Lauderdale, FL 33309

Marinco Electrical Products: Electrical products, 415-883-

3347, One Digital Drive, Novato, CA 94949
Marine Corporation Of America: Engines, 317-738-9408, 980 Hurricane Road, Franklin, IN 46131
MerCruiser: Engines, 405-743-6704, Stillwater, OK 74075
Micrologic: Electronics, 818-998-1216, 20801 Dearborn Street, Chatsworth, CA 91311
New England Ropes, Inc.: All types of line, 508-999-2351, Popes Island, New Bedford, MA 02740
Onan: Gensets, 612-574-5000, 1400 73rd Ave. N.E., Minneapolis, MN 55432
Origo, InterCon Marketing Inc.: Stoves and Refrigeration Kits, 1121 Lewis Ave., Sarasota FL 34237.
Paneltronics: Electrical Panels, 305-823-9777, 11960 NW 80th Ct, Hialeah Gardens, FL 33016
Poly-Planar Inc.: Waterproof Marine Speakers, Box 2578, Warminster, PA 18974. Webiste www.polyplanar.com.
Powerline: Alternators and Controls, 1-800-443-9394, 4616 Fairlane Ave, Ft Worth, TX 76119
R&R Textiles: Custom Deck Mats, 800-678-5920, 503-786-3678, 5096 Hwy. 76, Chatsworth, GA 30705. Web site www.rrrtextiles.com.
Racor Division-Parker Hannifin Corporation: Fuel Filters, 800-344-3286, P O Box 3208, Modesto, CA 95353
Raritan Engineering Company, Inc.: Heads, Treatment Systems, Charging Systems, 609-825-4900
Ray Jefferson Company: Electronics, 215-487-2800, Main & Cotton Sts., Philadelphia, PA 19127
Raytheon Marine Company: Electronics, 603-881-5200, 46 River Road, Hudson, NH 03051
Resolution Mapping: Electronic Charts and Software, 617-860-0430, 35 Hartwell Ave., Lexington, MA 02173
Sea Recovery Corporation: Water Purification, 213-327-4000, P O Box 2560, Gardena, CA 90247
Seagull Water Purification Systems: Water Purification, 203-384-9335, P O Box 271, Trumbull, CT 06611
SeaLand Technology: Marine Heads, 800-321-9886 or 330-496-3211, Fax 330-496-3097, P. O. Box 38, Big

Prairie, OH 44611.

Star Brite: Coatings/Sealants, 305-587-6280, 4041 S W 47th Ave., Ft. Lauderdale, FL 33314

Statpower Technologies Corp: Chargers, Inverters, 7725 Lougheed Hwy, Burnby, BC, Canada V5A 4V8

Teak Deck Systems: Teak Deck Caulking, 813-377-4100, 6050 Palmer Blvd., Sarasota, FL 34232

The Guest Company, Inc.: Electrical Components, Chargers, Inverters, 203-238-0550, P O Box 2059, Station A, Meriden, CT 06450

Trace Engineering: Chargers, Inverters, 206-435-8826, 5917 195th N.E., Arlington, WA 98223

U-Line Corporation: Ice Maker and Refrigeration, 414-354-3000, fax 414-354- 7905, Web site www.u-line.com, E-mail u-line@execpc.com, P O Box 23220, Milwaukee, WI 53223.

Unlimited Quality Products: Noise Reduction, 602-462-5235, 800-528-8291, 710 W. Broadway Rd #508, Mesa, AZ 85210.

Upholstery Journal/Marine Textiles: Magazine, P O Box 14268, St. Paul, MN 55114.

Vanner Weldon Inc.: Inverters & Chargers, 614-771-2718, 4282 Reynolds Dr., Hilliard, OH 43026-1297

Vermont Country Store: Table Cloths, P O Box 3000, Manchester Ctr., VT 05255

Webasto Heater, Inc.: Cabin Heaters, 313-545-8770, 1458 East Lincoln, Madison Hts., MI 48071

Westerbeke: Engines, 617-588-7700, Avon Industrial Park, Avon, MA 02322

Woolsey/Z-Spar: Paint, Varnish, Coatings, 800-221-4466, 36 Pine St, Rockaway, NJ 07866

Yanmar Diesel America Corp.: Engines, 708-541-1900, 901 Corporate Drive, Buffalo Grove, IL 60089-4508

APPENDIX FOUR
TOOLS & SUPPLIES

This list has been compiled through the joint effort of our staff and many contributing writers.

As you delve deeper into boating, you will always find a need for one more tool, or a few more supplies. It is truly a case of "Too much is never enough and enough is always too much." With this in mind it is best to adapt the following to your boat's needs and storage capacity.

The boat tools should not be shared with the car or the home. Purchase a good quality plastic tool box larger than the current need. Remove the handle which will certainly come off when you are transferring the box to the boat or the dock. A second box for less used tools is also a good idea.

* Tools for a small cruising sailboat without electrical or plumbing systems.

** Tools to add to the list for a mid-sized cruiser with electrical, plumbing, electronics and an inboard engine.

*** Tools for the long-term cruiser or liveaboard sailor intending to make most of the repairs to most of the systems.

The balance of the list will be needed at your land base for extensive repairs, renovations, upgrades and restoration projects.

HAND TOOLS

Good brands will carry a life time warranty.
* # 1, #2, #3 Phillips screwdrivers.
* Thin blade 3/16", medium blade 1/4", heavy blade 3/8" straight screwdrivers.
All the above should also be purchased in the stubby length.
** Jewelers set of screwdrivers.
** Various square drivers if you have this type of fastener on your boat. You will have to know the sizes you will need.
* Linesman pliers.
** Dikes/side cutters.
** Wire strippers. Buy the type with the stripper portion before the hinge.
** Terminal crimps.
** Digital multi-meter.
* Long-nose pliers.
** Needle-nose pliers.
* Vise Grips
* Small slip joint pliers (opens to 2").
*** Straight blade sheet metal cutters.
** Caulk gun.
*** Lufkin folding rule with brass slide extension.
** Large and small metal files.
* Set of allen wrenches 1/16" to 7/16" minimum.
*** China bristles paint brushes with an angle cut, in sizes 1", 1-1/2", 2", 2-1/2".
** School pencils.
** Pencil sharpener.
** Thin blade awl.
* 8" & 12" adjustable wrench.
** 12" Lenox hacksaw with 18, 24, & 32 teeth per inch blades.
** Estwing leather handle straight claw hammer.
*** A #2, & #3 nail set.
** Combination wrench set.
** 1/4" drive socket set.

* 3/8" drive socket set.

** Ignition wrench set.

The term "set" is used because most of these tools are sold in sets. You can purchase them individually but you will spend more than buying a set.

** 24" to 36" adjustable wrench. The size will depend on the prop nut size of your boat.

** Battery carrying strap.

** Feeler gauges (blade type).

** Cordless drill with two batteries, charger, cobalt drill bits ranging from 1/32" to 3/8" and screwdriver bits with a good holder. These should be the same size as your hand screwdrivers.

** Large slip joint pliers (opens to 4").

*** 2# Ballpeen hammer.

Caulking iron.

*** Rubber mallet.

*** Small & large Wonder bars.

*** Diston small dovetail saw.

*** Diston coping saw.

*** Diston 13 point hand saw.

*** Stanley 25' tape measure.

*** Stanley combination square.

*** Stanley #40 wood chisels 1/2", 3/4", 1".

These are the only Stanley tools you should own.

*** Block plane.

*** Half round wood file/rasp.

*** Heavy blade awl.

*** Larger size drill bits 7/16" to 1" forsener bits are the best for large wood bits. Metal bits should be cobalt.

*** Brad point bits 1/16" to 3/8".

Plug cutters 3/8" to 3/4"

*** Hole saw set.

*** Metal chisel and drift set.

** Right angle-straight and Phillips screwdrivers.

** Fish tape.

** Heavy gauge terminal crimp tool.

** Line wrench set.

** 1/2" drive socket set.

** Deep well socket set for all the different size drives you now own. Some of these may have been included when you purchased the sets.

*** 1/2" Breaker bar.

*** 1/2" Click stop torque wrench.

** 1/2" drive large sockets for all the bolts/nuts which are larger than the sets contain.

** Wrenches for the same bolts/nuts.

POWER TOOLS

Purchase brand name, heavy duty, commercial grade tools with a high ampere draw. These are the only tools that will last.

3/8" & 1/2" power drills.

Circular saw with good carbide tooth blades.

*** Random orbiting sander with 5" & 6" pads. Buy your 3M gold sanding disk in the 6" size and cut them down when you need the 5" size. Buy rolls of these grits. 60, 80, 100, 120, 150, 180.

Power miter box with an 80 tooth carbide blade.

3" x 24" or 4" x 24" belt sander. Buy at least three belts of each of these grits. 36, 80, 100, 120.

*** Soldering gun with electrical solder and flux.

Heat gun.

*** Random orbit buffer if you own a fiberglass boat.

Scrolling jigsaw with various wood and metal blades.

Router with various bits purchased as the jobs warrant. Always use roller bearing bits where applicable.

*** Sawz-all with various size and types of blades for wood/metal.

Biscuit jointer with at least two hundred of the two larger size biscuits.

*** 25', 50', & 75' #12 wire extension cords.

Table or radial arm saw. The radial arm saw can be set up with a multitude of attachments to handle many different functions other than cross cutting and ripping.

SUPPLIES
All Stainless Steel Fasteners

** At least 50 each of these Phillips head screws.

#4 x 1/2", 3/4", 1" Flat and oval head.

#6 x 1/2", 3/4", 1", 1-1/4", 1-1/2", 1-3/4", 2" Flat and oval head.

#8, #10, #12 Same as #6 plus 2-1/2", 3" Flat and oval head.

** Finish washers for each of the above size screw numbers.

#6, #8, #10, 1/2", 3/4", 1", 1-1/2" Pan head.

** At least 10 each of these fasteners.

1/4" x 20 x 2", 3", 4" Flat and stove head bolts with 2 washers and 1 nut each.

5/16" & 3/8" x 1", 1-1/2", 2", 2-1/2", 3" machine bolts with 2 washers and 1 nut each.

** Cap nuts for each of the above sizes.

*** 1/4" x 2", 3", 4", 5" lag bolts with washers.

** Large fender washers for each of the above sizes.

*** 2 pieces of solid rod 3' long in 1/4", 3/8", 1/2".

*** 2 pieces of threaded rod 3' long with 6 nuts and washers per piece in 1/4", 3/8", 1/2".

* Various size cotter pins to replace ones which will need to be removed. Check the sizes you need before ordering or purchase a cotter pin kit with various sizes included.

18 gauge brass or stainless steel brads in 1/2", 3/4", 1"

ELECTRICAL

** Butt terminals, male and female quick disconnect terminals. Order at least 50 each for wire gauges, 22-18, 16-14, 12-10, 8.

** Spade connectors, stud connectors. Order at least 50 each for the same gauge of wire above to fit around stud sizes 4-6, 8-10, 1/4", 5/16", 3/8".

*** 10 terminals for each size battery cable in use on your boat.

** 6 battery clamps (lugs, the kind used on your car) with stud. Do not connect the battery wires directly to the clamp; use the stud and terminals.

** 200 each of 6" & 11" medium duty wire ties.

*** 100 each of 3/4" and 1-1/2" cable clamps.

*** 1 each 4, 6, 8, 10 position terminal blocks. 6 each 20 amp in-line fuse holders with 5 each of, 5 amp, 10 amp, 15 amp, & 20 amp fuses.

*** 100 ft each of wire gauges 18, 16, 14, 12, 10, 8. Tinned marine primary wire.

*** 25 ft each of wire gauges 6 & 4.

*** 10 butt connectors for 6 & 4 wire.

*** 10 ft of battery cable for each size you have in use on board.

*** 2 ft each of heat shrink tubing 3/16", 1/4", 3/8", 1/2," 3/4".

MISC. ELECTRICAL SUPPLIES

** Liquid electrical tape.

** Vinyl electrical tape.

** Nylon string to use as a wire fishing device.

** 1 Pair of battery jumper cables. They must be long enough to reach between the banks of batteries you may need to jump. If you can not find them this long, make up your own with heavy ends and # 2 battery cable.

** Jumper wires for testing. These can be made with 4 alligator clips and 12 gauge wire.

** 1 breaker or fuse holder for each different size and type you on have board.

** 1 fuse for each specialty fuse on board.

** 1 switch for each type on board.

** 2 extra bulbs for each type on board.

** 1 lamp socket for each type on board.

*** 1 of each shore line end or an extra 50' shore line set.

** 1 connector for each type of electronic instrument connector on board.

SEALANTS, PAINT AND REPAIR PRODUCTS

** 1 tube each of Teak Deck Systems, 3M 5200 in white, GE silicone in white & clear, Star Bright polysulfide underwater sealant, Sea Repair.

** 1 small kit each of Epoxy, Marine Tex, Boat Yard fiberglass with 6 oz. cloth and matching gel coat colors.

*** 1 qt each of varnish, top sides paint for each color on board, stain, paint thinner, acetone, lacquer thinner, Penatrol, boiled linseed oil.

*** Coffee cans.

*** Plastic pots in 1 qt size.

*** Disposable brushes in 1/2", 1", 1-1/2", 2", 2-1/2".

PLUMBING PARTS

* The best method of determining your needs for plumbing will be to go through your supply and waste systems measuring each hose, clamp, tubing and fitting type and size. With this list in hand purchase at least two of each type of fitting, 10 of each size clamp, hose to replace the longest length of each size or fittings and hose to patch in the very long lengths. As with your shore power line, carry an extra water supply hose of no less than 50'. Also purchase water hose repair ends.

** This may not be considered plumbing by some, but it carries water, therefore it is included in this section. Your engines have many small sizes and lengths of hoses. As with the plumbing hoses, buy enough to replace the longest length of each size with the proper size clamps. These should be the heavy wall hose with wire reinforcement.

** If you have large exhaust lines you do not need to

carry a full length. Do carry a large coffee can with 4 hose clamps which are a larger size than the exhaust hose. You must carry at least one spare impeller or a rebuilding kit with the impeller included for every pump on board. THIS IS A MUST!

MISC. SUPPLIES

* Shock cords and ends.
* Buckets.
* Sponges.
* Chamois.
** Toilet brush.
** Scrub brush.
** Deck brush with handle.
*** Roller handle, pan and pads.
** Bronze wool.
** Bronze scrub brush.
** Detergents.
** Cleaning products.
** Polishes.
** Compounds.
** Water resistant/proof glue.
*** Extension cord ends.
** Patching material for every inflatable on board.
** Repair parts for engine(s).
*** Antifreeze.
** Oils.
** Grease gun with grease.
** Transmission fluid.
* 5 gals of extra fuel.
* Duct tape.
* Riggers tape.
*** Masking tape.
*** Sheet sand paper in grits 50, 80, 100, 120, 150, 180, 220.
     At least 5 sheets of each grit.
* At least two complete sets of dock lines and anchor rodes.

GLOSSARY

This glossary has been compiled through a joint effort of the staff of Bristol Fashion Publications and many authors. It is not intended to cover the many thousands of words and terms in the language exclusive to boating. The longer you are around boats and boaters, the more of this language you will learn.

A

Accumulator tank - A tank used to add air pressure to the freshwater system thus reducing water pump run time.

Aft - Near the stern.

Amidships - Midway between the bow and the stern.

Antifouling - Bottom paint used to prevent growth on the boat bottom.

Athwartships - Any line running at a right angle to the fore/aft centerline.

B

Backer plate- Metal plate used to increase the strength of a through bolt application, such as with the installation of a cleat.

Ballast - Weight added to improve a boat's sea handling abilities of the boat or to counterbalance an unevenly loaded boat.

Beam - The widest point of the boat.

Bilge - The lowest point inside a boat.

Bilge pump - Underwater water pump used to remove water

from the bilge.

Binnacle - A box or stand used to hold the compass.

Bolt - Any fastener with any head style and machine thread shank.

Boot stripe - Contrasting trim paint of a contrasting color located just above the bottom paint on the hull sides.

Breaker - Replaces a fuse to interrupt power on an electrical circuit when that circuit becomes overloaded or shorted.

Bridge - The steering station of a boat.

Brightwork - Polished metal or varnished wood aboard a boat.

Bristol Fashion - The highest standard of condition any vessel can obtain and the highest state of crew seamanship. The publishing company that brought you this book.

Bulkhead - A wall running across (athwartships) the boat.

Butt connectors - A type of crimp connector used to join two wires end to end in a continuing run of the wire.

C

Canvas - A general term used to describe cloth used for boat coverings. A type of cloth material.

Carlin - A structural beam joining the inboard ends of deck beams that are cut short around a mast or hatch.

Cavitation - Reduced propeller efficiency due to vapor pockets in areas of low pressure on the blades. Turbulence caused by prop rotation that reduces the efficiency of the prop.

Centerboard - A hinged board or plate at the bottom of a sailboat of shallow draft. It reduces leeway under sail.

Chafing gear - Any material used to prevent the abrasion of another material.

Chain - Equally sized inter-looping oblong rings commonly used for anchor rode.

Chain locker - A forward area of the vessel used for chain storage.

Chine - The intersection of the hull side with the hull bottom, usually in a moderate-speed to fast hull. Sailboats and displacement-speed powerboats usually have a round bilge and do not have a chine. Also, the turn of the hull below the waterline on each side of the boat. A sailboat hull, displacement hull and semi-displacement hull have a round chine. Planing hulls all have a hard (sharp corner) chine.

Chock - A metal fitting used in mooring or rigging to control the turn of the lines.

Cleat - A device used to secure a line aboard a vessel or on a dock.

Clevis - A Y-shaped piece of sailboat hardware about two to four inches long that connects a wire rope rigging terminal to one end of a turnbuckle.

Coaming - A barrier around the cockpit of a vessel to prevent water from washing into the cockpit.

Cockpit - Usually refers to the steering area of a sailboat or the fishing area of a sport-fishing boat. The sole of this area is always lower than the deck.

Companionway - An entrance into a boat or a stairway from one level of a boat's interior to another.

Cribbing - Large blocks of wood used to support the boat's hull during it's time on land.

Cutlass Bearing® - A rubber tube that is sized to a propeller shaft and fits inside the propeller shaft strut.

D

Davit - Generally used to describe a lifting device for a dinghy.

Delaminate - A term used to describe two or more layers of any adhered material that have separated from each other because of moisture or air pockets in the laminate.

Device - A term used in conjunction with electrical systems. Generally used to describe lights, switches receptacles, etc.

Dinghy - Small boat used as a tender to the mother ship.

Displacement - The amount of water, in weight, displaced by the boat when floating.

Displacement Hull - A hull that has a wave crest at bow and stern and settles in the wave trough in the middle. A boat supported by its own ability to float while underway.

Dock - Any land based structure used for mooring a boat.

Draft - The distance from the waterline to the keel bottom. The amount of space (water) a boat needs between its waterline and the bottom of the body of water. When a boat's draft is greater than the water depth, you are aground.

Dry rot - This is not a true term as the decay of wood actually occurs in moist conditions.

F

Fairing - The process of smoothing a portion of the boat so it will present a very even and smooth surface after the finish is applied.

Fairing compound - The material used to achieve the fairing process.

Fairlead - A portion of rigging used to turn a line, cable or chain to increase the radius of the turn and thereby reduce friction.

Fall - The portion of a block and tackle system that moves up or down.

Fastening - Generally used to describe a means by which the planking is attached to the boat structure. Also used to describe screws, rivets, bolts, nails etc. (fastener)

Fiberglass - Clothlike material made from glass fibers and used with resin and hardener to increase the resin strength.

Filter - Any device used to filter impurities from any liquid or air.

Fin keel - A keel design that often resembles an up-side-down "T" when viewed from fore or aft.

Flame arrestor - A safety device placed on top of a gasoline carburetor to stop the flame flash of a backfiring engine.

Flat head - A screw head style that can be made flush with or recessed into the wood surface.

Float switch - An electrical switch commonly used to automatically control the on-off of a bilge pump. When this device is used, the pump is considered to be an automatic bilge pump.

Flying bridge - A steering station high above the deck level of the boat.

Fore - The front of a boat.

Fore-and-aft - A line running parallel to the keel. The keel runs fore-and-aft.

Forecastle - The area below decks in the forwardmost section. (pronunciation is often fo'c's'le)

Foredeck - The front deck.

Forward - Any position in front of amidships.

Freeboard - The distance on the hull from the waterline to the deck level.

Full keel - A keel design with heavy lead ballast and deep draft. This keel runs from the bow, to the stern at the rudder.

G

Galley - Kitchen.

Gelcoat - A hard, shiny coat over a fiberglass laminate that keeps water from the structural laminate.

Gimbals - A method of supporting anything that must remain level regardless of the boat's attitude.

Grommet - A ring pressed into a piece of cloth through which a line can be run.

Gross tonnage - The total interior space of a boat.

Ground tackle - Refers to the anchor, chain, line and connections as one unit.

H

Hanging locker - A closet with a rod for hanging clothes.

Hatch - An opening with a lid that open in an upward direction.

Hauling - Removing the boat from the water. The act of pulling on a line or rode is also called hauling.

Hawsehole - A hull opening for mooring lines or anchor rodes.

Hawsepipes - A pipe through the hull, for mooring or anchor rodes.

Head - Toilet. Also refers to the entire area of the bathroom.

Helm - The steering station and steering gear.

Holding tank - Used to hold waste for disposal ashore.

Hose - Any flexible tube capable of carrying a liquid.

Hull - The structure of a vessel not including any component other than the shell.

Hull lines - The drawing of the hull shape in plan, profile and sections (body plan).

I

Inboard - Positioned toward the center of the boat. An engine mounted inside the boat.

K

Keel - A downward protrusion running fore and aft on the center line of any boat's bottom. It is the main structural member.

King plank - The plank on the center line of a wooden laid deck.

Knees - A structural member reinforcing and connecting two other structural members. Also, two or more vertical beams at the bow of a tugboat used to push barges.

L

Launch - To put a boat into the water.

Lazarette - A storage compartment in the stern of a boat.

Lead - The material used for ballast.

Limber holes - Holes in the bilge timbers to allow water to run to the lowest part of the bilge, where it can be pumped out.

LOA - Length Over All. The over all length of a boat.

Locker - A storage area.

Log - A tube or cylinder through which a shaft or rudder stock runs from the inside to the outside. The log will have a packing gland (stuffing box) on the inside of the boat. Speed log is used to measure distance traveled. A book used to a keep record of the events on board a boat.

LWL - Length on the Waterline. The length of a boat at the water line.

M

Manifold - A group of valves connected by piping to tanks to allow filling and removal from one or more tanks.

Marine gear - Boat's transmission.

Mast - An upward pointing timber used as the sail's main support. Also used on power and sailboats to mount flags, antennas and lights.

Mile - A statute mile (land mile) is 5280 feet. A nautical mile (water mile) or knot is 6080.2 feet.

Mizzen mast - The aftermost mast on a sailboat.

N

Nautical mile - A distance of 6080.2 feet

Navigation lights - Lights required to be in operation while underway at night. The lighting pattern varies with the type, size and use of the vessel.

Nut - A threaded six-sided device used in conjunction with a bolt.

Nylon - A material used for lines when some give is desirable. Hard nylon is used for plumbing and rigging fittings.

O

Oval head - A screw head used when the head can only be partially recessed. The raised (oval) portion of the head will remain above the surface.

Overhangs - The length from the bow or stern ending of the waterline to the forward or aft end of the hull.

P

Painter - A line used to tow or secure a small boat or dinghy.

Pan head - A screw head with a flat surface, used when the head will remain completely above the surface.

Panel - A term used to describe the main electrical distribution point, usually containing the breakers or fuses.

Pier - Same general use as a dock.

Pile - A concrete or wooden post driven or otherwise embedded into the water's bottom.

Piling - A multiple structure of piles.

Pipe - A rigid, thick-walled tube.

Planing hull - A hull design, which under sufficient speed, will rise above it's dead-in-the-water position and seem to ride on the water.

Planking - The covering members of a wooden structure.

Plug - A type of pipe, tubing or hose fitting. Describes any device used to stop water from entering the boat through the hull. A cylindrical piece of wood placed in a screw hole to hide the head of the screw.

Port - A land area for landing a boat. The left side when facing forward.

Propeller (Prop, Wheel, Screw) - Located at the end of the shaft. The prop must have at least two blades and propels the vessel through the water with a screwing motion.

R

Radar - A electronic instrument which can be used to "see" objects as blips on a display screen.

Rail - A non-structural safety member on deck used as a banister to help prevent falling overboard.

Reduction gear - The gear inside the transmission housing that reduces the engine rpm to a propeller shaft Rpm that is optimum for that hull and engine.

Ribs - Another term for frames. The planking is fastened to these structural members.

Rigging - Generally refers to any item placed on the boat after the delivery of the vessel from the manufacturer. Also refers to all the wire rope, line, blocks, falls and other hardware needed for sail control.

Ring terminals - A crimp connector with a ring that can have a screw placed inside the ring for a secure connection.

Rode - Anchor line or chain.

Rope - A term that refers to cordage and this term is only used only on land. When any piece of cordage is on board a boat, it is referred to as line or one of it's more designating descriptions.

Round head - A screw or bolt head with a round surface that remains completely above the material being fastened.

Rudder - Located directly behind the prop and used to control the steering.

Rudder stock - Also known as rudder post. A piece of round, solid metal attached to the rudder at one end and the steering quadrant at the other.

S

Samson post - A large piece of material extending from the keel upward through the deck and used to secure lines for mooring or anchoring.

Screw - A threaded fastener. A term for propeller.

Screw thread - A loosely spaced, coarse thread used for wood and sheet metal screws.

Sea cock - A valve used to control the flow of water from the sea to the device it is supplying.

Shackle - A metal link with a pin to close the opening. Commonly used to secure the anchor to the rode.

Shaft - A solid metal cylinder that runs from the marine gear to the prop. The prop is mounted on the end of the shaft.

Shear pin - A small metal pin that inserted through the shaft and propeller on small boats. If the prop hits a hard object, the pin will "shear" without causing severe damage to the shaft.

Sheaves - The rolling wheel in a pulley.

Sheet metal screw - Any fastener that has a fully threaded shank of wood screw threads.

Ship - Any seagoing vessel. To ship an item on a boat means to bring it aboard.

Shock cord - An elastic line used to dampen the shock stress of a load.

Slip - A docking space for a boat. A berth.

Sole - The cabin and cockpit floor.

Spade rudder - A rudder that is not supported at its bottom.

Stability - The ability of a hull to return to level trim after being heeled by the forces of wind or water.

Stanchion - A metal post that holds the lifelines or railing along the deck's edge.

Starboard - The right side when facing forward.

Statute mile - A land mile. 5280 feet.

Stem - The forwardmost structural member of the hull.

Step - The base of the mast where the mast is let into the keel or mounted on the keel in a plate assembly.

Stern - The back .

Strut - A metal supporting device for the shaft.

Stuffing box -T he interior end of the log where packing is inserted to prevent water intrusion from the shaft or rudder stock.

Surveyor - A person who inspects the boat for integrity and safety.

Switch - Any device, except breakers, that interrupts the flow of electrical current to a device.

T

Tachometer - A instrument used to count the revolutions of anything turning, usually the engine, marine gear or shaft.

Tack rag - A rag with a sticky surface used to remove dust before applying a finish to any surface.

Tank - Any large container that holds a liquid.

Tapered plug - A wooden dowel tapered to a blunt point and is inserted into a seacock or hole in the hull in an emergency.

Tender - A small boat (dinghy) used to travel between shore and the mother ship. A boat with limited stability is said to be tender.

Terminal lugs - Car-style, battery cable ends.

Through hull (Thru hull) - Any fitting between the sea and the boat that goes "through" the hull material.

Tinned wire - Stranded copper wire with a tin additive to prevent corrosion.

Topsides - Refers to being on deck. The part above the waterline.

Torque (or Torsion) - The rotating force on a shaft. (lb-in)

Transmission - Refers to a marine or reduction gear.

Transom - The flat part of the stern.

Trim - The attitude with which the vessel floats or moves through the water.

Trip line - A small line made fast to the anchor crown. When weighing anchor this line is pulled to back the anchor out and thus release the anchor's hold in the bottom.

Tubing - A thin-walled metal or plastic cylinder, similar to pipe but having thinner walls.

Turn of the bilge - A term used to refer to the corner of the hull where the vertical hull sides meet the horizontal hull bottom.

Turnbuckles - In England, they are called bottle screws. They secure the wire rope rigging to the hull and are used to adjust the tension in the wire rope.

V

Valves - Any device that controls the flow of a liquid.

Vessel - A boat or ship.

VHF radio - The electronic radio used for short-range (10 to 20 mile maximum) communications between shore and vessels and between vessels.

W

Wake - The movement of water as a result of a vessel's movement through the water.

Washer - A flat, round piece of metal with a hole in the center. A washer is used to increase the holding power of a bolt and nut by distributing the stress over a larger area.

Waste pump - Any device used to pump waste.

Waterline - The line created at the intersection of the vessel's hull and the water's surface. A horizontal plane through a hull that defines the shape on the hull lines. The actual waterline or just waterline, is the height at that the boat floats. If weight is added to the boat, it floats at a deeper waterline.

Water pump - Any device used to pump water.

Wheel - Another term for prop or the steering wheel.

Whipping - Any method used, except a knot, to prevent a line end from unraveling.

Winch - A device used to pull in or let out line or rode. It is used to decrease the physical exertion needed to do the same task by hand.

Windlass - A type of winch used strictly with anchor rode.

Woodscrew - A fastener with only two-thirds of the shank threaded with a screw thread.

Y

Yacht - A term used to describe a pleasure boat, generally over twenty-five feet. Usually used to impress someone.

Yard - A place where boats are stored and repaired.

INDEX

Building A Fiberglass Boat by Arthur Edmunds

Books published by
Bristol Fashion Publications
Free catalog, phone 1-800-478-7147

Boat Repair Made Easy — Haul Out
Written By John P. Kaufman

Boat Repair Made Easy — Finishes
Written By John P. Kaufman

Boat Repair Made Easy — Systems
Written By John P. Kaufman

Boat Repair Made Easy — Engines
Written By John P. Kaufman

Standard Ship's Log
Designed By John P. Kaufman

Large Ship's Log
Designed By John P. Kaufman

Designing Power & Sail
Written By Arthur Edmunds

Building A Fiberglass Boat
Written By Arthur Edmunds

Buying A Great Boat
Written By Arthur Edmunds

Boater's Book of Nautical Terms
Written By David S. Yetman

Practical Seamanship
Written By David S. Yetman

Captain Jack's Basic Navigation
Written By Jack I. Davis

Creating Comfort Afloat
Written By Janet Groene

Living Aboard
Written By Janet Groene

Racing The Ice To Cape Horn
Written By Frank Guernsey & Cy Zoerner

Marine Weather Forecasting
Written By J. Frank Brumbaugh

Complete Guide To Gasoline Marine Engines
Written By John Fleming

Complete Guide To Outboard Engines
Written By John Fleming

Complete Guide To Diesel Marine Engines
Written By John Fleming

Trouble Shooting Gasoline Marine Engines
Written By John Fleming

Trailer Boats
Written By Alex Zidock

Building A Fiberglass Boat by Arthur Edmunds

Skipper's Handbook
Written By Robert S. Grossman

White Squall - The Last Voyage Of Albatross
Written By Richard E. Langford

Cruising South
What to Expect Along The ICW
Written By Joan Healy

Five Against The Sea
A True Story of Courage & Survival
Written By Ron Arias

Scuttlebutt
Seafaring History & Lore
Written By Captain John Guest USCG Ret.

Cruising The South Pacific
Written By Douglas Austin

Catch of The Day
How To Catch, Clean & Cook It
Written By Carla Johnson

VHF Marine Radio Handbook
Written By Mike Whitehead

Building A Fiberglass Boat by Arthur Edmunds

ABOUT THE AUTHOR

Arthur Edmunds graduated from the U.S. Coast Guard Academy and completed his military service. After working at shipyards for a short time, he was a working designer for a leading boat manufacturer. He opened his design office in 1968 and has been busy ever since with a great variety of projects, not specializing in any type of boat or hull form. Repairs, rebuilding and engineering consultation have formed a large part of the design business. He believes in prowling boat repair yards where every problem in the world of boating is exposed for all to see and learn. Finding what goes wrong and what materials are best for a certain application is a very necessary part of a designer's portfolio.

He has crewed on ocean racing sailboats but also appreciates most people prefer to go maximum speed in powerboats. Successful designs have been completed for both manufacturers and individuals in all materials, and in all hull shapes. He has been residing in Florida since 1960 and now lives in Sarasota, FL.

Everyone hears strange and funny anecdotes about boats and men and Edmunds has a few tales to tell. He was standing near a tall, muscular winch grinder at an after race party who was mesmerizing a sweet young thing. The girl said she was amazed the spinnaker was set so high and wondered how it was done. The grinder happily replied, "We use spray starch."

CPSIA information can be obtained at www.ICGtesting.com
Printed in the USA
LVOW121748110112

263410LV00002B/42/A

9 781892 216168